Content Literacy

An Inquiry-Based
Case Approach

Elizabeth G. Sturtevant
George Mason University

Wayne M. Linek
Texas A&M University–Commerce

PEARSON

Merrill
Prentice Hall

Upper Saddle River, New Jersey
Columbus, Ohio

Vice President and Executive Publisher: Jeffery W. Johnston
Editor: Linda Ashe Montgomery
Editorial Assistant: Laura Weaver
Production Editor: Mary M. Irvin
Design Coordinator: Diane C. Lorenzo
Text Design and Production Coordination: Holly Henjum, Carlisle Publishers Services
Cover Designer: Eric Davis
Cover Image: Corbis
Production Manager: Susan Hannahs
Director of Marketing: Ann Castel Davis
Marketing Manager: Darcy Betts Prybella
Marketing Coordinator: Tyra Poole

This book was set in New Baskerville by Carlisle Communications, Ltd. It was printed and bound by R. R. Donnelley & Sons Company. The cover was printed by Coral Graphics.

Photo Credits: All photos provided by authors.

Pearson Education Ltd.
Pearson Education Singapore Pte. Ltd.
Pearson Education Canada, Ltd.
Pearson Education—Japan

Pearson Education Australia Pty. Limited
Pearson Education North Asia Ltd.
Pearson Educación de Mexico, S.A. de C.V.
Pearson Education Malaysia Pte. Ltd.

10 9 8 7 6 5 4 3 2 1
ISBN: 0-13-526691-2

Dedicated to
Dave, Paul, Lee, Daniel, and Jessica
and
Laura, Jenny, Barry, and Adrienne
For their love, patience, and support

Foreword

Content Literacy: An Inquiry-Based Case Approach is a book that I always wanted to write, but didn't. Fortunately for the literacy education field, Betty Sturtevant and Wayne Linek, two of my former students, did. This book represents the missing link in the literature on content literacy. Not only are the authors very much in step with where the field of adolescent/content literacy is situated today, they also combine qualitative research techniques embedded in a case study framework to produce an invaluable instructional resource for preservice and inservice teachers.

Through the inquiry-based case approach that they take, Betty and Wayne fill a void and add an important dimension that heretofore has been absent in content literacy textbooks. Up to this point, content literacy textbooks have followed a topical approach, developing various aspects of content literacy instruction and engaging readers in strategy explanations, models and demonstrations, and research/theory-based discussions. This book, however, takes the proverbial "road less traveled." It adheres to an inquiry-based case format that "shows" rather than "tells" its readers what constitutes effective content literacy practices. And that makes all the difference in its potential impact and contribution to the field.

Rather than providing strategy explanations supported by research and theoretical underpinnings, the authors invite us to study real teachers working with real students. The teachers represent different content areas, different instructional styles, and different beliefs about teaching and learning. Yet what they have in common is a concern for the literacies that their students bring to content instructional situations—and a commitment to scaffolding instruction in ways that support literacy and learning. As readers of this book, you will feel like you are sitting in the back of their classrooms observing the teachers as they plan and deliver instruction as well as grapple with problems that arise in the context of teaching. Someone once said that nothing is as practical as a good theory. Betty Sturtevant and Wayne Linek's book suggests that nothing is as theoretical as a good practice.

On the one hand, the authors make a unique contribution to the content literacy field; yet through the Content Area Handbook, they bridge what traditionally has been offered in more traditional text formats (e.g., strategy explanations). The combination of in-depth case studies and easily accessible strategy explanations is a powerful tool for inquiry and problem-solving discussions in content literacy courses. Like I said earlier, I wish I'd had the foresight to write this book, but then you would be missing out on what's ahead for you. As readers, you are in for a treat. The teachers you are about to study are wonderful models of what it means to teach strategically. Not only do they know the *what* and *how* of content literacy, but they also know the *when* and *why* of instructional practice. The underlying structure to each case will allow you to make cross-comparisons among the teachers, identifying problems common across teachers and problems unique to each teacher.

For me, teaching has always been a problem-solving activity. There are no pat formulas, no stock lessons, no single strategy that will make a difference in the literate lives of your students. There's just you, the text(s) that you use, and the students whose lives you touch in the brief time that they are under your wing. Teaching is a daunting enterprise for those who are up to the challenge. Studying how other teachers have met the challenge will make you a better teacher.

Richard T. Vacca, Professor Emeritus
Kent State University

About the Authors

Elizabeth Sturtevant is an associate professor at George Mason University in Fairfax, Virginia, where she teaches courses in literacy education and serves as co-coordinator of the Literacy Program Area. Previously a high school reading specialist, middle school social studies teacher, and community college developmental education instructor, Betty earned her Ph.D. from Kent State University. She currently is an editor of the *Journal of Literacy Research* and was a co-editor of the College Reading Association Yearbook for 8 years. She also is co-chair of the International Reading Association's Commission on Adolescent Literacy. Betty has conducted research on adolescent literacy and teacher development. She has published numerous book chapters and articles in journals including *Reading Research and Instruction,* the *Journal of Literacy Research,* the *NASSP Bulletin,* the *Journal of Educational Research,* the *National Reading Conference Yearbook,* and the *College Reading Association Yearbook.*

Wayne Linek is a professor at Texas A&M University-Commerce, where he teaches courses in content area literacy and research design; he also serves as coordinator of the Supervision, Curriculum, and Instruction Doctoral Program. Previously an elementary teacher, middle school teacher, reading specialist, and administrator, Wayne earned his Ph.D. from Kent State University. He currently is an editor of the *Journal of Literacy Research* and serves as president of the College Reading Association. He also was a co-editor of the College Reading Association Yearbook for 8 years. Wayne has conducted research on teacher education and literacy. He has published numerous book chapters and articles in journals such as *Reading Research and Instruction, Language Arts,* the *Journal of Educational Research, Reading Horizons,* the *National Reading Conference Yearbook,* and the *College Reading Association Yearbook.*

Preface

Helping adolescents develop the skills and knowledge they need for school and life is a challenge faced by all middle and high school teachers. In addition to mastering content knowledge in a wide variety of disciplines, teenagers need to develop *content literacy*, or the ability to learn effectively through reading, writing, and discussion, in every content area. Teachers who plan instruction that facilitates both content knowledge and literacy learning can have a strong impact on their students' current and future success.

Many preservice and practicing teachers, however, have difficulty using strategies designed to increase students' content literacy because they have never seen or experienced this type of methodology in their own education. This book employs a *case study* approach that helps teachers imagine and implement theory-based instruction by bringing them into the classrooms of actual 6th through 12th grade teachers in a variety of subject areas. The teachers and teacher teams highlighted in the cases connect reading, writing, and oral communication with content learning in a wide variety of ways. Each case provides a situated and holistic view of teaching and gives insight into teachers' personal histories, planning, and instructional decision making.

ORGANIZATION OF THE TEXT

The text begins with an introduction that explores the concept of content literacy and how instruction in this area is essential for meeting adolescents' learning needs. Readers are provided with essential background information on literacy, constructivist philosophy, and adolescent learning and development. A "thought question" helps readers to begin thinking about what the concept of content literacy might mean for their own discipline. This is followed by the International Reading Association's Position Statement on Adolescent Literacy (Moore et al., 1999) as well as additional information on relationships among literacy, language, and learning; the value of student inquiry; and why content teachers are best suited to work with students on content literacy.

The introductory chapter also briefly explores cultural and institutional constraints at the middle and secondary school levels that have historically affected teachers' ability to implement various theory-based practices. For example, rigid time blocks and heavy content coverage requirements often are cited by teachers as roadblocks to including reflective discussion in their instruction. The purpose of this description is to provide readers with background to help them understand various dilemmas reported by teachers in the following chapters and to assist them in conceptualizing solutions to common problems.

The introductory chapter ends with a suggested format that readers can use to analyze each case. This chart mirrors charts provided in the final chapter and Content Area Handbook that enable readers to conduct a cross-case analysis after reading all of the chapters.

Chapters 2 through 8 present authentic cases of teachers or teams of teachers in a wide variety of content disciplines in two regions of the United States. The teachers, who were recommended by principals, supervisors, and university professors, are working to put theory into practice. The teachers themselves, their school settings, students, and instruction are described in a narrative format. Dilemmas the teachers face in their instructional decision making, their perceptions of how they have changed through the years, and ways they hope to modify their instruction in the future are also described. In this way, teaching is presented as a reflective decision-making process that develops and changes over time rather than as a static enterprise.

The final chapter of the text has a teacher researcher emphasis. Readers are encouraged to compare and contrast the cases in the text with one another. They also are provided with a framework for observing teachers in their own regions and comparing what they observe with what they have read in the text.

SPECIAL FEATURES

Additional pedagogical features of the book include the content literacy strategies in which readers are immersed during study of each chapter as well as the Content Area Handbook at the end of the text that presents numerous practical resources as well as directions for further study. Each chapter begins with a thought question and a theory-based content literacy strategy that readers can use *before, during,* and *after reading*. Discussion questions that can be used for reflection by individuals, groups, or a whole class are also provided. These questions and strategies can help readers develop in-depth understandings of concepts presented; they also serve as models of different types of content literacy strategies.

Overall, we intend this as both a theoretical and practical text that will enable readers to gain a multifaceted view of content literacy so that they can effectively put this concept to work in their own classrooms. The text also provides support for teachers' growth as inquirers into the process of teaching adolescents by offering a structure for case analysis, observations in the field, and other resources.

ACKNOWLEDGMENTS

Many people have helped and encouraged us during the lengthy development of this text. First, we wish to thank the teachers and students described throughout the text who gave so much of their time and insight as case participants. The teachers included Becky Adams, Leslie Rush, Karen Shepherd, Gene Zablotney, Millie Mennard, Sri Viswanathan, Mark Crossman, Kris Martini, Maureen Noonan-Moore, Cathy Hix, Bonnie Loriz, Julie Dickson, Patricia Baron, Elizabeth Clevenger, and Nicole Jones. Each welcomed us into their classroom and spent many days with us, helping us understand how they connected literacy and content learning.

In addition, our graduate assistants have provided tremendous support with case study and book development over several years. These individuals have included Marlene Darwin, Carla Deniz, Vicki Duling, Sylvia Perez-Fasano, Judith Fontana, Jill Jenkins, Eileen McCartin, Joanna Newton, Gail Ritchie, Vicky Spencer, and Julie Tiss at George Mason University, as well as Kim Klakamp, Michelle Fazio, Syam Sundar and Charlene Fleener at Texas A&M University-Commerce.

We also are indebted to our editors at Merrill/Prentice Hall, including Brad Potthoff, who inspired us to initiate the project, and Linda Montgomery, who gently pushed us to publication. We wish to thank the reviewers, including Judith L. Irvin, Florida State University; William Kist, Kent State University; Michael McKenna, Georgia Southern University; Kouider Mokhtari, Loyola Marymount University; Edith A. Norris, West Texas A&M; Denise H. Stuart, The University of Akron; and Richard Vacca, Kent State University.

Finally, we especially thank Nancy Padak, Timothy Rasinski, and Richard Vacca (Kent State University), our mentors and dear friends. Through their modeling we learned to collaborate.

Educator Learning Center:
An Invaluable Online Resource

Merrill Education and the Association for Supervision and Curriculum Development (ASCD) invite you to take advantage of a new online resource, one that provides access to the top research and proven strategies associated with ASCD and Merrill—the Educator Learning Center. At **www.EducatorLearningCenter.com** you will find resources that will enhance your students' understanding of course topics and of current educational issues, in addition to being invaluable for further research.

HOW THE EDUCATOR LEARNING CENTER WILL HELP YOUR STUDENTS BECOME BETTER TEACHERS

With the combined resources of Merrill Education and ASCD, you and your students will find a wealth of tools and materials to better prepare them for the classroom.

Research

- More than 600 articles from the ASCD journal *Educational Leadership* discuss everyday issues faced by practicing teachers.
- A direct link on the site to Research Navigator™ gives students access to many of the leading education journals, as well as extensive content detailing the research process.
- Excerpts from Merrill Education texts give your students insights on important topics of instructional methods, diverse populations, assessment, classroom management, technology, and refining classroom practice.

Classroom Practice

- Hundreds of lesson plans and teaching strategies are categorized by content area and age range.
- Case studies and classroom video footage provide virtual field experience for student reflection.
- Computer simulations and other electronic tools keep your students abreast of today's classrooms and current technologies.

LOOK INTO THE VALUE OF EDUCATOR LEARNING CENTER YOURSELF

Preview the value of this educational environment by visiting **www.EducatorLearningCenter.com** and clicking on "Demo." For a free 4-month subscription to the Educator Learning Center in conjunction with this text, simply contact your Merrill/Prentice Hall sales representative.

Contents

Foreword   iv

About the Authors   vi

Preface   vii

PART I   AN INTRODUCTION TO CONTENT LITERACY   1

chapter 1   Teaching, Learning, and Growing With Adolescents   1

A Book of Case Studies   2

   Making Connections   2

   Focus on Content Literacy   3

   What This Book Is Not   3

   Thought Questions   3

   What Does It Mean to Be Content Literate?   4

   How Do Different Fields View Content Literacy?   4

Adolescents, Literacy, and Learning   5

   Understanding Adolescence   5

   Adolescence and Literacy   5

   Adolescence and Literacy Instruction   6

   IRA Principles on Adolescent Literacy   6

   Teachers' Responsibility   7

Exploring Inquiry Learning Through Cases   10

PART II   CONTENT LITERACY: CLASSROOM CASE STUDIES   11

chapter 2   Sixth Grade World History   11

Meeting Becky   14

Inside Becky's Classroom   14

A Close Look at Instruction   16

    Making Instructional Decisions   17

    Research Beyond Her Community   18

    Teaching and Learning Strategies   18

    Reading, Writing, and Oral Communication   20

    Textbooks and Materials   20

    Grouping Arrangements   20

    Special Projects and Assignments   22

Working and Growing as a Professional   24

Concerns   26

Summing Up   27

chapter 3 The S. S. Toy Company Project: Grade Seven   28

Background   30

    Seventh Grade Collaboration   31

The S. S. Toy Company   31

    First Steps   31

    In Process   32

    The Simulation Experience   32

    Student Reflections   35

    Teachers' Reflections   36

Summing Up   38

chapter 4 Integrated Civics and English: Grade Eight   40

Meeting Millie and Gene   42

Inside Millie and Gene's Classroom   43

    Beginning the Year   43

    Making Connections   44

    Moving Forward   45

    Community Involvement   46

The Volunteerism Unit   46

    Planning and Beginning   48

    Student Efforts   48

    Uses of Language   49

    Bringing It All Together   49

Synthesis and Extension   52

Assessment   54

Conversations with Gene and Millie   54
  On Teaming   54
  On Students   56
  Facing Challenges   56
Staying Current   57
Summing Up   57

chapter 5   **High School Biology**   59

Meeting Karen   60
Inside Karen's Classroom   61
  Overall Goals   62
  Awareness of Student Needs   62
A Close Look at Instruction   63
  Planning and Instructional
    Decision-Making   63
  Focus on Literacy   64
  Focus on Written Communication   66
  Focus on Discussion   66
  Sensitive Topics   67
  Modifications for Special Needs   70
Working and Growing as a Professional   70
Concerns   72
  Motivation   72
  Staying On Schedule   72
  Time Management and Student Responsibility   73
  Dilemmas in Selecting Teaching Strategies   74
Summing Up   74

chapter 6   **High School Mathematics**   75

Meeting Sri   76
Inside Sri's Classroom   77
A Close Look at Instruction   78
  Connections and Concepts   79
  Expanding Understanding   80
Special Projects and Assignments   80
  Algebra I: The Slope Project   80
  Functions: The Time Zone Project   82
  Project Assessment   84

Group Assignments   85
Working as a Professional   88
Concerns   89
Summing Up   90

chapter 7   High School English   92

Meeting Leslie   93
Inside Leslie's Classroom   94
A Close Look at Instruction   95
Scaffolding New Experiences   96
Focus on Discussion   97
Strategic Teaching and Learning   98
Emphasis on Writing   99
Modifications for Special Needs   101
Special Projects and Assignments   101
Working as a Professional   103
Concerns   104
Summing Up   105

chapter 8   English for Speakers of Other Languages   107

Meeting Mark   108
Inside Mark's Classrooms   109
A Close Look at Instruction   111
Linking Writing, Reading,
and Personal History   112
Special Projects and Assignments   118
Working as a Professional   119
Concerns   120
Summing Up   120

PART III   PLANNING FOR ACTION RESEARCH   122

chapter 9   Reflecting on Teaching and Learning   122

Looking Back: What Adolescents Deserve   123
Looking Forward: Teaching as Inquiry   124
Taking a Stance as a Teacher Researcher   125
Final Thoughts   127

PART IV   RESOURCES FOR CONTENT LITERACY INSTRUCTION   129

Content Area Handbook   129

Teaching and Learning Strategies Referenced in Chapters   131

Brainstorming   132

Categorization and Word Maps   132

Discussion Web   134

Double Entry Journals   135

DR-TA or Directed Reading-Thinking Activity   136

Graphic Organizers (*see* Semantic Mapping)

INSERT (Interactive Notation System to Effective Reading and Thinking)   138

K-W-L   139

LINK (List, Inquire, Note, Know)   141

Post-Graphic Organizer   142

Prediction   142

PreP (Pre Reading Plan)   143

Progressive Cinquain   144

Progressive Writing   145

Save the Last Word for Me   145

Semantic Mapping and Graphic Organizers for Expository Text Structure   146

Sketch to Stretch   153

Summarization   153

Think–Pair–Share   154

Webbing (*see* Semantic Mapping)

Word Maps (*see* Categorization)

Your Own Questions   155

References for Teaching and Learning Strategies   155

National Standards and Goals   157

Additional Suggestions for Case Analyses and Field Experiences   167

Additional References, Resources, and Websites   172

References   177

Index   179

chapter 1

Teaching, Learning, and Growing With Adolescents

This book will take you into middle and high school content area classrooms. Five teachers and two teacher teams are portrayed with a particular focus on ways they include literacy and communication strategies in their teaching. The teachers vary in age, gender and ethnicity; they teach different subjects; they live and work in different regions of the United States. Despite this diversity, these teachers have developed some common ideas about teaching and learning. One similarity is that they believe that learning happens as students work with ideas and use reading, writing, discussion, and classroom experiences in purposeful, strategic ways (Sturtevant, 1996). Although the teachers use various terms to describe what they do, many of their teaching methods can be defined as content literacy strategies, because they encourage the use of reading, writing, and discussion for learning in a content discipline (McKenna & Robinson, 1990).

Importantly, these teachers also are known as people who take a wonderfully positive and creative approach to their work with adolescents. While not immune to the substantial pressures on teachers everywhere, they enjoy teaching and remain committed to their own growth as both teachers and learners. They also are known as excellent teachers of their disciplines. While not "perfect" teachers (there are none!), they are well regarded both within and beyond their own schools.

As any teacher knows, teaching is a multi-dimensional, complex human endeavor that cannot be reduced to lists or sets of instructions. Studies of teaching going back over 30 years have found that teachers must be highly adaptable decision makers with a strong knowledge base in many areas (Jackson, 1968). Middle and secondary teachers, for example, must have a firm grasp of both their content areas and the complexities of adolescent development. They also must know how to apply this knowledge to create productive classroom environments that support and inspire young people's learning and growth. This is, to say the least, no easy task.

Developing true competence as a teacher requires both a lifelong commitment to learning and repeated opportunities to study and reflect on our own and others' experiences as teachers. Learning to teach is a process and does not happen overnight. Like a successful family physician or athletic trainer, the teacher must be both a scholar/scientist who understands the workings of the human body and mind and a coach who knows how to apply this knowledge on a day-to-day basis.

A BOOK OF CASE STUDIES

Case studies can play an important role in professional growth for both beginning and more experienced teachers. In our view, good teaching does not require choosing between abstract theories presented in traditional textbooks and the concrete examples of "practice" we can observe in schools. Rather, both are valuable resources for developing the in-depth knowledge base that professional teachers need to make informed decisions. Yet, it sometimes is difficult for both new and experienced teachers to connect the two. Observations in any local area are necessarily limited to the teaching practices and contexts available, and textbook descriptions of "best practice" are often difficult to envision and apply. As narratives about real individuals and events that are linked to research and theory, written cases can become an important means of bridging different forms of knowledge. Case studies can bring us into the lives and classrooms of teachers we probably will never meet. They also can provide a starting point for individuals or groups of teachers who wish to reflect upon and discuss ideas or dilemmas related to teaching. In essence, case studies can add an important dimension to a teacher's efforts to grow professionally.

Making Connections

We write this book from a *constructivist* view of learning, in that we hope it will help readers connect new ideas to their own past experiences, beliefs, and knowledge (Philips & Cleverley, 1995). We also advocate that teachers consider the cognitive, social, and political dimensions of their own teaching and learning (Hynds, 1997). Classrooms are affected by a wide variety of influences, both personal and cultural. These influences will be explored here as we meet each teacher or team of teachers and observe both differences and similarities in their backgrounds, beliefs about instruction, and constraints and opportunities present in their teaching contexts.

As you read, consider how these classrooms are similar to or different from what you have experienced in your lifetime. Also consider how you might apply what is presented to your own teaching, now or in the future. We urge you to think beyond the text, connect the text with your knowledge from other readings or experiences, and apply what you discover in your own setting.

Each chapter provides thought questions to consider before you begin reading, a framework for analyzing each case, discussion strategies, and suggested activities. Information on conducting your own teacher researcher project is included in the final chapter.

Focus on Content Literacy

As noted earlier, a major goal of this text is to help teachers of every discipline gain a deeper understanding of content literacy, or the ways reading, writing, and discussion can support and extend learning in their content areas. We interviewed teachers with this goal in mind. However, we also seek to *situate*, or imbed, the descriptions of content literacy instruction within the larger context of a teacher's instruction. This is important because content literacy strategies, or any other teaching methods, never occur in isolation. They are always part and parcel of the larger fabric of instruction in a particular setting.

As you read, you will be encouraged to use some content literacy strategies yourself. Explanations of these strategies are provided in the Content Area Handbook at the back of the text. Teachers have told us that "trying out" strategies helps them get a real sense of how they "work," or "don't work" for themselves as learners. While studying these cases as an adult reader is not the same as reading a content text in chemistry might be for a secondary school student, "trying out" strategies can enhance a teacher's feeling for what students may experience.

What This Book Is Not

This book is not a comprehensive catalog of content literacy strategies. As you may know, dozens of content literacy strategies and suggested practices have been developed. While this text describes a variety of these strategies that are useful in different content areas, you may find you need additional information on particular strategies. We have provided a list of resources to help you find this information in the Handbook at the end of this book. Our assumption is that readers will have access to a variety of publications and resources in addition to this book, in order to gain a full perspective of the range of strategies that might be useful in their own situations.

This also is not a book about "perfect" teachers. While one of our goals was to seek well-respected teachers who see themselves as learners, the teachers portrayed here would be the first to say that they are still learning as teachers—that as professionals, their own "learning to teach" is never finished. If you could meet these individuals, they would invite you, whatever your experience or inexperience as a teacher, to learn *with* them. Use their experiences as resources to assist you in meeting the needs of your own students and situation, but do not try to exactly copy or replicate what you read here. Each teacher is different, and each context and group of students is different.

Thought Questions

Each chapter will begin with a "thought question" or activity to provide readers an opportunity to consider their own prior knowledge and instructional beliefs. Before continuing in this introductory chapter, we invite you to reflect on your own views about literacy and learning.

Thought Question for Chapter 1   Brainstorm a definition of content literacy as it relates to your subject area. In other words, if you are, or plan to be, a math teacher, what does it mean to be content literate in mathematics? Why do you think so? You may want to make notes on your response and discuss your ideas with others, before reading further.

Write your definition of *content literacy* for your subject area here:

What Does It Mean to Be Content Literate?

What was your definition of *content literacy*? What thinking processes did you consider? Did you include reading, writing, and other uses of language? In what ways do you think background knowledge or knowledge in a particular discipline contributes to an individual's content literacy? Researchers who explore literacy and learning have used the term *content literacy* to encompass all of these ideas (Vacca & Vacca, 2002). In essence, over the past twenty-five years, literacy has been found to be a very complex concept, reaching far beyond traditional notions of decoding words, interpreting sentences, or finding main ideas in paragraphs. While the term *literacy* is most often used in relation to reading and writing, content literacy also relates to conceptual understanding and background knowledge in a content discipline. For example, "computer literate" has come to mean an understanding of computers, while the term "scientific literacy" is used to indicate knowledge of science concepts. We all use our content literacy to learn new concepts by connecting what we already know to new information we encounter.

How Do Different Fields View Content Literacy?

In the past 20 years, the research base that supports our knowledge of oral and written language development, linguistics, psychology, and other areas related to literacy has expanded greatly. Educators also have studied ways to more effectively teach mathematics, science, social studies, and other curricular areas, which has led to the development of National Standards documents in a wide variety of disciplines. Most of these National Standards (see Handbook for summaries) concur about the value of inquiry-based experiential forms of learning combined with group discussion, reading of relevant, interesting materials, and written reflection and synthesis.

In *Best Practice*, Zemelman, Daniels, and Hyde (1993) called this emerging consensus among traditionally separated fields of study a "coherent philosophy and spirit . . . [that is] . . . reaching across the curriculum and up through the grades" (p. 7). While recommendations for this type of curriculum are not new, during the past thirty years an expanded research base in cognition and human learning has provided a depth of support that was not previously available (Zemelman, Daniels, & Hyde, 1993). The standards also serve as food for thought so that you can compare and contrast what you see in each case with the standards provided by the "experts." But how do the standards connect to adolescents, learning, and teaching?

ADOLESCENTS, LITERACY, AND LEARNING
Understanding Adolescence

In order to effectively teach adolescents, it is important to first gain an understanding of who they are. If your knowledge of adolescence is limited to your own passage through this period of life, we recommend that you take every opportunity to update and expand your knowledge, by studying and observing adolescents both in and out of school settings.

Over the past 30 years, the authors of this book have worked with both adolescents and teachers of adolescents in a variety of school and university settings. We have also recently experienced adolescence as parents of adolescent children. Like many teachers we know who work in middle and high schools, we find that we really enjoy teenagers, at least much of the time. The very qualities that can make adolescence a difficult age can also make working with young people in this age group very rewarding.

Adolescents, like all learners, are diverse in a wide variety of ways. Each is a unique individual, yet also a member of one or more groups or cultures. They often exhibit different types or uses of literacy (sometimes called *multiple literacies*) in different settings. Their motivation may also vary tremendously across different types of projects—when hooked on an idea, commitment, or cause, they may work devotedly. But the same individual may, at other times, or for other projects, exhibit total apathy or do only what is necessary to get by. This can be exasperating for both teachers and parents and confusing to adolescents themselves.

Adolescence and Literacy

Like their differences in other areas, adolescents have vast differences in what is called "literate behavior." Do you remember your own adolescence as a time of incessant reading, maybe in hidden spots such as an old apple tree or in a particular room of the public library? Or do you recall never touching a book during those years, especially a textbook? Like many other adolescents, perhaps you read only what was absolutely required, with a stash of *Cliffs* notes and maybe an occasional Shakespearean movie to prepare for a test.

While a variation in motivation and learning is a normal part of the adolescent growth process, educators have found that particular types of instruction are especially likely to inspire adolescent interest. This book explores ways teachers at the middle and high school levels can capitalize on adolescents' natural propensity for using language for learning. For example, one key relates to the opportunity for *choice*, or personal decision making that adolescents are given about what they learn and how they learn it. Many teachers find that adolescents value opportunities to select their own reading materials or topics for research (Gambrell, 1995). In essence, while young people at this age need guidance, they also need to feel they are beginning to control their own destinies.

What does "literacy" mean, when thinking about the adolescent learner? We expect teachers of young children to devote time to helping them become literate. However, it often is assumed that once students pass into the middle grades they will have "learned to read" and teachers will be able to turn their attention to "content." This is a misperception on two counts. First, the teachers of young children can and do teach content at the same time their students are learning to read. Plus, teachers can be of tremendous help to their older students when they continue to plan for students' literacy needs. This holds true, *even if students are academically advanced.*

Adolescence and Literacy Instruction

While "everyone knows" that young children need literacy instruction, it is less accepted or understood that adolescents need thoughtful instruction and coaching in order to continue in their development as readers and writers. The need for guidance is not the result of failures in teaching or learning during the preschool or primary years; it is an important part of normal literacy development. Thus, guiding adolescents to advanced levels of literacy ought to be a critical portion of the curriculum in middle and secondary schools (Moore, Bean, Birdyshaw, & Rycik, 1999). Guidance is needed across subject areas so that sophisticated reading and writing abilities develop as adolescents increase their knowledge of the world, oral language vocabulary, and thinking abilities.

IRA Principles on Adolescent Literacy

To guide efforts to put concepts of adolescent literacy learning into practice, the Commission on Adolescent Literacy of the International Reading Association (IRA) developed seven principles for supporting adolescents' literacy growth (Figure 1-1). IRA developed these principles partly because middle and secondary school curriculums sometimes emphasize content learning so much that literacy development is ignored. True content literacy in a subject area, however, must be modeled by an expert in that subject area—the content area teacher. The understanding that one is responsible for content literacy in one's subject area becomes clear when considering the results reported in the National Assessment of Educational Progress (NAEP) Reading Report Card (2002). This report documents, for example, that although the majority of 8th graders in the United States (approximately 73%) could comprehend text containing specific factual information, only 3% could extend or elaborate upon the meaning of the material read, and only 2% could write essays expressing "analytical, critical, and/or creative thinking" (http://nces.ed.gov/nationsreportcard/writing/achieveall.asp). This is disturbing information since adolescents entering the 21st century "Information Age" will be required to read and write more than any other time in human history.

Research has shown that literacy is not one skill or ability, but an array of ways people can communicate (Richardson & Morgan, 2003). Literacy is a powerful but sometimes overlooked tool. Adolescents need literacy—both now, when they are growing and changing, and in preparation for their futures. For example, society today requires highly developed literacy skills of all people, from using e-mail to completing complex tax forms. On the other hand, literacy demands are changing. While voice recognition computer programs may make reading somewhat less

FIGURE 1-1 Seven Principles of International Reading Association's Position Statement on Adolescent Literacy

1. Adolescents deserve access to a wide variety of reading material that they can and want to read.
2. Adolescents deserve instruction that builds both the skill and desire to read increasingly complex materials.
3. Adolescents deserve assessment that shows them their strengths as well as their needs and that guides their teachers to design instruction that will best help them grow as readers.
4. Adolescents deserve expert teachers who model and provide explicit instruction in reading comprehension and study strategies across the curriculum.
5. Adolescents deserve reading specialists who assist individual students having difficulty learning how to read.
6. Adolescents deserve teachers who understand the complexities of individual adolescent readers, respect their differences, and respond to their characteristics.
7. Adolescents deserve homes, communities, and a nation that will support their efforts to achieve advanced levels of literacy and provide the support necessary for them to succeed.

Source: Position Statement on Adolescent Literacy, International Reading Association, 1999. (http://reading.org/positions/adol_lit.html)

essential in the future, Internet connections mean that masses of information are available that must be sorted through. One must be content literate to access, analyze, and critically evaluate this flood of information.

Teachers' Responsibility

A teacher's responsibility for developing content literate students in the classrooms of today goes far beyond imparting basic content knowledge. In our view, an ideal curriculum focuses on processes based in a search for understanding. Students can inquire, explore, discover, and think critically as they meet their own personal information needs. Thus, an understanding of how to use reading, writing, and discussion as tools for learning becomes the goal of the content area classroom. This stance helps to prepare students to function as thinking citizens who can effectively protect individual liberty in a democratic society.

The power of literacy has internal dimensions as well. Through well-written stories, humans can travel into new spaces where they can vicariously experience alternate worlds, learn about ideas from others' perspectives, try out new ways of thinking, and rehearse ideas. Technological advances now allow people to interact with numerous others, in faraway countries or close to home. Content teachers in the middle and high schools can play a truly vital role in helping students develop their literacy abilities and use them for learning across a lifetime.

FIGURE 1-2   Case Analysis Chart Phase One [To Be Completed at the End of Every Chapter]

Most interesting parts of the case:

What I liked best and my reason:

What I disagreed with (or what caused dissonance for me) and my reason:

Teacher, event, or situation it reminded me of in my own school experience:

What I saw that related to student motivation:

What I saw that related to student engagement:

What I saw that related to classroom organization:

What I saw that related to teaching approaches:

What I saw that related to meeting student needs:

What I saw that related to incorporation of literacy in the content area:

Ideas or strategies I could apply in my own teaching situation:

EXPLORING INQUIRY LEARNING THROUGH CASES

This book has an overall focus on inquiry learning, or ways that both teachers and students can become involved in asking and answering their own questions related to issues of importance to them, including (but certainly not limited to!) teaching, learning, and areas of school curriculum (Brubacher, Case & Reagan, 1994). As you read the cases in this book, be alert to the ways that students are using literacy and language as part of an inquiry process, to understand, extend, and explain their experiences. For example, in chapter 4, Millie and Gene, an English/civics teacher team in Virginia, ask 8th grade students to explore volunteerism in their community. Over several weeks, the students locate and contact community volunteers, write questions to ask, conduct audiotaped interviews, transcribe the tapes, use the tapes as primary source documents in class discussions, write summaries, create group diagrams and illustrations, and communicate their findings to the community in a wall display. Throughout this process, Gene helps students connect the new information with civics concepts learned earlier in the year. Students also are continuously strengthening their use of language processes, which is the content of Millie's English curriculum.

We hope that as part of your own inquiry into teaching and learning you will read these cases, analyze them, reflect on them, and then discuss them with your colleagues. Which parts are most interesting? What types of lessons did you like and which ones bothered you, and why? Have you met teachers like these? Which ideas or strategies could you apply to your teaching situation, or apply with some creative modification?

The chart in Figure 1-2 provides a framework for studying, analyzing, and discussing each case. Completed charts for each chapter can be used in a cross-case analysis that is described in the final chapter.

To begin your case analysis, look at one category on the chart at a time. Keeping that category in mind, review the case and take notes that describe the personal characteristics, beliefs, and practices of the teacher or teachers in that case. For example, in the case in chapter 2, Becky uses time on computers and the Internet for motivation. She encourages students to listen to the news and has them share what they believe is important, which may relate to student engagement, and so on. Begin work on phase one of your case analysis and discuss your findings for each category with colleagues in your school or class. Later, you can complete phase two, which involves making a cross-case comparison. This is described in the final chapter.

Overall, we suggest you take the stance of an action researcher or learner who views a situation through multiple lenses. The text will provide an avenue for reflection on different teachers' perspectives, histories, contexts, and decisions.

Although we suggest that you use this framework as an aid for reflection with every chapter, there are likely to be additional concepts or topics you will find important in your own observations. We know that the cases will undoubtedly leave as many questions unanswered as answered, because that is how teaching is. There are no easy answers.

chapter 2

Sixth Grade World History

GUIDELINES

Thought Questions Consider the following questions and note your answers in a log or journal.

1. What connections do you make when you hear the phrase "sixth grade social studies"?
2. What do you see as major rewards or challenges of teaching middle school students?

- Before reading, you may want to engage in a content area literacy strategy. We suggest the *LINK Strategy* (see description in the Content Area Handbook, p. 141). This strategy helps readers link their background knowledge to the reading material.
- While reading this chapter you may wish to use the *Insert Strategy*, discussed in the Handbook (p. 138). This strategy helps readers interact with the text and clarify their thinking as they read.
- National Standards in Social Studies can be found at: http://peabody. vanderbilt/edu/depts/tandl/faculty/Myers/standards/html

It's 10:15 A.M., the bell rings and it is time to change to third period class on this Wednesday morning. Becky takes her place by the door as students are spilling into the hall, stopping at their lockers and chatting about the latest edition of *What's Up In Sixth Grade: News by Students for Students* (see Figure 2-1).

"Did you see that bit in the paper about the Bubonic Plague? Gross! Hey Ms. A., can I come in after school today to e-mail my pen pal in Italy? I'm working on an article about Leonardo Da Vinci and I want to see if Licia knows something about him that I don't." Becky has the crowded schedule in her hand and helps Austin find an open spot during a tutorial/enrichment period later that week.

Justin angles for Becky's attention and says, "Ms. A., I listened to the news this morning and I've got an 'On This Day in History' to share." Becky nods approvingly and asks Justin to be ready to discuss his news item with the class.

As the other students step into the room they notice a white glove hanging over the door. "Ms. A., what's that white glove doing over the door?" Vanessa asks. Becky chuckles and says, "That's something I'd like you to find out. It's one of our challenges for the next unit."

Once inside, students check out the bulletin board where items for "Trivia," a "Quote of the Day" and "On This Day in History" are posted. They read the instructions on the blackboard for their warm-up activity, which includes reading an article in the *Medieval Chronicle* in old English.

As the bell rings, Becky asks students to share their thoughts about the quote of the day, "Nothing great is ever achieved without enthusiasm." There are lots of volunteers. Students talk about the importance of a positive attitude and doing your best. Then Becky asks Justin to share what he heard on the early morning news.

Next she asks if anyone can summarize the article from the *Medieval Chronicle* "in a nutshell," but there are no volunteers. Becky asks what the problem is, and students say that it's "hard to read the funny looking print" and that they "don't know the words." Becky explains that language and writing styles change through history, and begins a vocabulary and concept development lesson on feudalism in her unit on the Middle Ages. Just before students leave for the day, Becky mentions that the white glove hanging over the door indicates an upcoming Medieval Festival that will be part of their new unit.

These classroom events took place at an intermediate school for over 500 fourth, fifth, and sixth grade students located in a small university town in northeast Texas. The town has a residential population of about 8,000, and about the same university population. The community includes widely diverse housing, and employment includes industry, farming, and the university.

Becky is a sixth grade teacher with responsibility for teaching world history. Her schedule includes six 45-minute world history classes per day that include a total of 130 students. She also has an additional period of tutorials and enrichment that is part of a building-wide student achievement initiative called "Zeros Aren't Permitted." This program is designed to enable all students to succeed and pursue their individual interests.

The sixth grade has its own wing of an expansive building. Students are heterogeneously grouped in classes ranging in size from 14 to 29 students. Becky indicates that the sixth grade has always been departmentalized because this grade was originally part of the junior high school. She believes it benefits sixth graders to change classes and "get the feel of junior high" before they go to the larger, two-story junior high building the next year.

Students in the school are culturally and economically diverse and have varying educational needs. All students in the district attend the same school for grades 4–6, and most students with special needs are included in regular classroom instruction.

WHAT'S UP IN SIXTH GRADE

Volume 3
News by students, for students

The Bubonic Plague
by: Kenny

In the Middle Ages there was a plague called the Bubonic Plague. The Bubonic Plague was brought to England by rats from ships docking in London and other places. This virulent and horrific disease spread quickly throughout the country, killing 68,596 people in a matter of months.

Infected families were boarded up in their homes and many took their own lives rather than suffer the torments of the disease, sewing themselves into their own shrouds, ready for the pits.

Project Keep Hope Alive
by: Jay

There is a new group in town called Keep Hope Alive. It is a program for African American young boys to help them learn. We step, go places and perform. We have shirts with our name on them. We learn new stuff everyday.

BRANDI

Brandi is a 13 year old girl in the 6th grade and her hobbies are fishing, swimming, horseback riding and being with her friends, but mainly sports...

She likes to play football & baseball and her favorite drink is Dr. Pepper. She likes pizza, but hates tuna salad and koolaid........yuck!!!!

by: Heather

Leonardo Da Vinci

Leonardo Da Vinci was born in 1452. He died in 1519. He drew hundreds of his own inventions and even dissected corpses to study. One of his most famous paintings was the Mona Lisa. He wrote his notes in mirror writing.   By: Austin

MUSIC

There are many different types of music. One of my favorite types of music is R & B. One of my favorite groups is Immature. They are very talented, and I love their new song "Please Don't Go." The song is the bomb. I have their posters all over my wall. I have 30 posters of them. I can't see how people can dislike music. Music is a part of me. Without music I don't know what to do.

By: Valorie

Spotlight on: Reggie

My spotlight is on Reggie.... formally known as < SUGAR BEAR >. He is 12 years old. His favorite foods are ice cream, grapes, and apples. His favorite drink is Gatorate. Sugar Bear likes to play sports. His hobbies are stepping, jogging, and playing board games.

by: KC

Spotlight on: Mandi

This spotlight is on Mandi. Her favorite color is blue. Her favorite sport is volleyball. Mandi says that when she grows up she wants to be a Social Studies teacher. BYE.

by: Kennesha

FIGURE 2-1   "What's Up In Sixth Grade" Student Newsletter

A variety of support services are available, including specialist teachers and a "content mastery" classroom where students may go for extra assistance. The school is a Title I school, which indicates that it receives additional federal funding due to a large low-income population.

MEETING BECKY

At the time of our interviews, Becky was in her sixth year of teaching sixth grade at her current school and her tenth year of teaching overall. She was teaching in the community where she grew up and attended college. Becky earned her initial degree in business and accounting. Prior to entering the field of education, she worked in Dallas for four years in the corporate offices of both Dr. Pepper and Pizza Hut. She notes that she had dreamed of becoming a teacher as a child, but in high school had an accounting teacher who was a "huge influence" on her and encouraged an interest in business. She was also attracted to the salaries in business, but later "didn't like [her] job that much" because she thought that all that she was doing was "helping the pocketbook of the owner" rather than "contributing in any way to society."

Becky returned to East Texas State University (now Texas A&M University–Commerce) and worked as a graduate assistant while getting her teaching certificate and master's degree simultaneously. She finished her program midyear and immediately began teaching first grade in a nearby rural community. The following school year she began teaching third grade at the primary school in the university town, moving three years later into her sixth grade position. Becky describes both the community and the university as supportive of the public schools.

Becky is glad she became a teacher and describes teaching as her "passion." She says she loves to see students get excited about learning and strongly believes teachers can become influential role models by demonstrating a love of learning and a respect for all learners. She comments that young adolescents have high expectations of their teachers and can "see right through teachers" who are insincere or unconcerned about students' needs. It is obvious that she works hard for her students and expects them to work hard as well.

INSIDE BECKY'S CLASSROOM

Walking into Becky's room, an observer sees small clusters of student desks in the center and eight computer stations spread out around the perimeter (see Figure 2-2). Several of the computers have Internet connections. The teacher's desk is off to one side, and holds a computer attached to a large monitor suspended from the ceiling for student viewing. Becky explains that she has more computers than other teachers in her school because she won a technology grant to support her instruction.

The walls and bulletin boards in the classroom are covered with photographs, student work, and other displays related to recent units of study. Interestingly, Becky also has arranged multiple clocks just below the ceiling that display the current time at various places in the world (see Figure 2-3).

When asked to give an overview of her instruction, Becky identified several critical goals that she focuses upon at the beginning of each year. First, she works to create a "risk-taking environment" where students are comfortable being themselves and are able to immerse themselves in learning. She says she has learned that accomplishing her goal of a positive classroom climate takes small but consistent steps. An example is her attitude toward student responses to her questions. "If

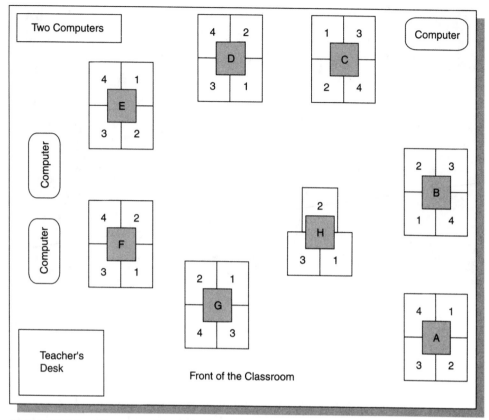

FIGURE 2-2 Diagram of Becky's Classroom

someone [gives] a wrong answer I try to take them in another direction and not make a big deal out of it so that they won't be afraid to speak out and try." Throughout the year, Becky also builds a positive environment through experiences that help students link their own lives with what is going on in school.

Becky thinks student motivation is extremely important, and notes that some teaching strategies build motivation better than others. In particular, she uses techniques that help her students connect areas of interest in their own lives with the sixth grade world history content. One strategy she uses involves creating different types of timelines. Early in the fall, students create timelines that begin with their own lifetimes. They write examples of major historical events that have occurred in each year of their lives on the timelines. Later, students expand their personal timelines to include events from both their parents' and an older family member's lifetime. Timeline expansion takes place again, during each unit of study, as students construct a timeline with the new historical information and combine it with their

FIGURE 2-3   Multiple Clocks Display Time Across the Globe

personal timeline. Becky has found through the years that this timeline strategy helps students gain historical perspective while maintaining personal connections to the content material.

Becky also thinks it is essential to help students set their own learning goals. She begins this process on the first day of school and continues throughout the year with student-made "world history passports." To get started, Becky shares her own United States passport and explains its purpose. She then has students create classroom passports using their thumbprints, personal photos, lists of desired destinations, and personal social studies goals for the year. Over the course of the year, she encourages students to revisit their passports to clarify their own interests and learning goals in relation to the history content presented in class.

A CLOSE LOOK AT INSTRUCTION

Becky's overall goals include teaching her students important social studies concepts as well as developing their competence in reading, writing, communication, and higher-order thinking. Like most teachers, she thinks it is essential to get off to a good start when beginning a school year. She notes:

> The first thing I try to do is to create good rapport with the kids. I've always enjoyed learning myself, so I try to relate that enthusiasm . . . and I try to teach, above all else, that learning is a lifelong process.

Becky finds she needs to plan carefully to accomplish her goals. Over the years, she has developed some strategies for planning that take her through the year. At the beginning of each year, she plans "very generally." Her goal at this stage is to set a classroom tone and help students make connections to one another and the new material. She also works to learn more about students' background knowledge and interests. After she sees "where the kids are moving" and what they need to learn, Becky plans the specifics of her units.

Making Instructional Decisions

When choosing topics and concepts to include, Becky has a range of options within the world history curriculum. She says she is "very fortunate" that her school district does not have a rigid curriculum for sixth grade world history that she is "told to teach." She notes that she is "left on [her] own to choose what's most important" and that she does this by taking the needs of her students and the nature of the content into consideration.

Becky's yearly plans include several units of study. For example, she often teaches units on ancient cultures such as Ancient Greece or Egypt (see Figure 2-4), as well as specific time periods, such as the Middle Ages. Some areas of study, such as the influence of religion on history, cross several units. Becky also includes the study of current world cultures through a special project in which students work in small groups to study countries they choose.

FIGURE 2-4 Egyptian Boat Model Created as Part of Special Small Group Project

Over several years, Becky has developed a pattern for the structure of her units. She usually introduces a unit by asking students to brainstorm what they already know in a modified K-W-L format. She then leads the class in a semantic mapping activity in which the whole group contributes ideas as Becky creates a map related to the new topic on the blackboard (see the Handbook for descriptions of K-W-L and semantic mapping). The timeline activity described earlier also helps students connect new information to their personal and family histories at the beginning of each unit. After Becky has made decisions about what concepts she will cover in a particular unit, based on the time available and her students' prior knowledge, she plans daily lessons and class projects.

Throughout the year, Becky uses a wide variety of reading and writing materials, including a course text, non-fiction and fiction books, and resources on Videodisk and the World Wide Web. She also includes oral communication activities, such as student presentations or debates based on student research. For example, in the unit on Rome students studied the role of gladiators and later held a debate on the ethics of gladiators' behavior. Becky videotaped the debate and other oral presentations so students could later evaluate their own presentations. She explained: "I like to video the kids doing simulations, role plays, those kinds of things, and to me, that builds not only their world history skills but their presentation skills."

When asked about how easily students learned complex debate skills, Becky noted that while some of her sixth graders seemed to "get up there and just argue for the sake of arguing" she really worked to "teach them to research and have good facts for the statements that they were making." She generally provides two or three days for research on a debate topic and requires students to have written lists of well-researched statements in advance.

Research Beyond Her Community

Another major goal Becky works to achieve is to help her young students gain a deeper understanding of cultures that may be very different from their own. She knows that many students who live in her small Texas town have only limited experience with people from different backgrounds. Becky works hard to brings in resources, including guest speakers, related to other parts of the world. For example, the class communicated by mail with a Scottish teacher Becky had met at a professional meeting. Later this individual visited the United States and came to see Becky's classes. In addition, during the study of the Middle East and the Islamic religion, Becky invited a student's father, who had visited the Middle East, to share information from his trip. He showed a Koran to the class and discussed aspects of Islamic belief and traditions. Students also communicated via e-mail with a classmate who had moved with her family to Saudi Arabia because of her parents' employment (see Figure 2-5). Becky says that she teaches with the aim that her students will examine their own biases and learn "that cultures other than their own are not 'weird,' just different."

Teaching and Learning Strategies

Throughout the year, Becky uses a variety of strategies designed to help students get the most out of their reading and studying. She finds that these techniques also

FIGURE 2-5 E-mail Message From Former Student Currently Living in Saudi Arabia

From: Kacy
To:
Subject: Hi Ms.A. and sixth grade
Hi, how is everyone there I'm fine. Saudi is cool it does have grass and trees. School here is about the same in the states except we do not get a chance to start it at school like yall do. Has anyone new come since I left? what are yall studing in all the classes. I will send yo a picture of me in my obya, if you send me a picture of the whole sixth grade so I can be remembered of everyone. I will also send you some of their money if you want me to. They are called Ryials and the coins are called Halalas. Here are my classes that I'm taking, Social Studies, Science, Math, English, Personal Finance, Lititure Review, and last but not least P.E. The hrdest one I think is Social Studies, because he makes us memorize the contries in Africa. Now that is hard, so no complaining about you have-hard work. Mrs. A. I knew more before I came than they did I'm doing stuff we did a long time ago. Like adding and subtracting Fractions: Reading and English are mixed here so that is only one class for me. We have Block Schduling . We only go to P.E. three times a week, and we don't even streghth really good. We run the mile at least once a week. It is werid because I have to go to school on Saturday and Sunday, but I don't have to go to school on Thursday and Friday. But I'm used to it know. I have met some friends but they all live on another Compound. I live in Taif, on a mountain called the Ascratment. Well ,don'have much more to say so Bye!! much more to say so Bye!!
Your Truly,
Kacy
P.S. Write back soon.

develop important reasoning skills students will need throughout life. Strategies she uses include modeling, writing process, and thinking/planning tools such as webs, Venn diagrams, and a K-W-L process. Her assessments of student learning are also varied so that she can get information on a variety of student competencies. She often uses a method called a "think aloud" to demonstrate a reading strategy for her students. She notes,

> Modeling is a big part of my teaching . . . [and] I try real hard to think out loud as much as I can and try to help them see what is most important so they can get to a point where they can make those decisions on their own.

A specific example of her use of strategies involves Venn diagrams (see Handbook). Becky's students made Venn diagrams to compare the democracy in ancient Greece with the United States government. First, the whole group brainstormed words and phrases describing the characteristics of each democracy. Students then independently completed Venn diagrams in their notebooks. Later they compared their diagrams with peers in their group and discussed similarities and differences. Finally the teacher led a whole class discussion that combined the insights of all students.

FIGURE 2-6 Student in Costume for Presentation on the Middle Ages

Reading, Writing, and Oral Communication

Becky also believes it is important to provide time for daily reading and writing in her classroom, as well as frequent opportunities for oral communication. Many aspects of class work include all three. For example, during the unit on the Middle Ages, Becky's students researched a topic or historical figure and then wrote scripts for a TV news story. Students rehearsed their scripts, and then were videotaped in costume (Figure 2-6). The video was later viewed by the other periods of social studies classes. Becky said, "This activity was very effective because [students] had to write their own scripts and they were extremely interested in what their peers in other classes had done." She did experience a time crunch with this activity, but felt students benefited tremendously even though she had to limit practice to one rehearsal. She also noted that she ran the video camera herself and only permitted one "take" per group.

Textbooks and Materials

Becky uses a variety of print materials as well as media and Internet resources. She believes that students learn more when they use multiple sources, and also notes that history texts go out of date very quickly: "[Until this school year] we had a textbook for 10 years or so and of course in world history with the maps and all that kind of thing, it grew out of date quickly. So, *Junior Scholastic* and [other resources] helped keep me current." Interestingly, Becky does not ignore the older maps, but keeps them on hand so that students can make comparisons with newer maps.

Becky has a variety of strategies to help students understand multiple viewpoints and gain information from sources beyond her textbook. For example, when students are doing research projects she normally brings a variety of books from the library into the classroom. Students also use encyclopedias, computer reference tools, and Internet sources. She conducts specific activities to help students use the technology in the classroom. For example, in the early part of the year she has students complete an activity called "Be a Tech Pro" to insure that they can use computers and basic software in the classroom (see Figure 2-7).

Grouping Arrangements

Throughout each unit, Becky's students work in a variety of group arrangements including individual, small group, and whole class. For example, when the class is

FIGURE 2-7 "Be a Tech Pro" Activity

Name:

Be a Tech Pro . . .
Being Proficient with Technology

Our goal in Social Studies is never to treat technology as a "separate subject" in our curriculum. We want to learn to use technology as a tool for our learning. Therefore, our goal is to help each other be proficient in using our technology available in order to be able to efficiently and effectively learn more about our global community.

Basic Technology Skills
- Show how to properly handle a disk
- Show the menu bar
- Explain what is meant by "under the apple"
- Show the multifinder
- Show the launcher
- Close the launcher
- Pull the launcher back up
- Show how to "hide" an application
- Show how to switch from one application to another, having two applications open at one time
- Show the desktop

Clarisworks . . .
- Open ClarisWorks word processing document
- Hide Claris Works
- Make ClarisWorks reappear
- Show the tool bar
- Type Commerce Tigers
- Center Commerce Tigers in the middle of the line
- Make the first letter of Commerce & Tigers size 24 font
- Make all the other letters of Commerce Tigers size 14 font
- Make your name bold, Cooper Black font
- Make your name italics
- Make your name red
- Put a football in the center of your page
- Make the football about 5" wide
- Draw a wide yellow rectangle around your football
- Make the inside of the rectangle orange
- View all of your document at one glance
- Write #1 on page 2 in size 72 font in orange color, shadow style
- Save your document on a disk and title it your first name
- Save your document on the desktop and title it your first name

learning to locate Internet sources on topics of interest, Becky often begins with a whole-class presentation using her computer, which is attached to a TV screen. After gaining an overview of the process, students then work in small groups to conduct searches using the classroom computers. During this time period, Becky circulates among groups to provide assistance. Students' final projects often include a mixture of individual and group assignments. These projects are often given both a group and individual grade.

Sometimes, Becky finds that she can use the technology in her room to best advantage by rotating groups among different "stations." Each computer is designated for a particular purpose or type of material, such as a World Wide Web search, or a program on a CD-ROM. Examples include *Time Almanac*, a biography program called "Faces", and other CD-ROMS related to news.

When asked how she created the groups that were working on the computers Becky said,

> I let the kids put down on a sheet of paper who they thought they would like to work with, and if there was someone in the class that they thought they absolutely could not work with. [However] I was very clear in telling them that those people might or might not be in their groups. For this particular project, I decided to do my groups fairly homogeneously.

In essence, Becky uses flexible grouping arrangements that she modifies for different types of activities. She finds that teaching with small groups enables her to make the best use of her resources and also enables students to participate actively in classroom experiences.

Special Projects and Assignments

Becky connects special projects to most of her units because she believes that permitting students to explore areas of interest adds to their motivation and increases their involvement with the subject matter and overall learning. Projects also enable students to apply their research skills, as they have to locate, read, and synthesize ideas from a wide variety of resources.

One of the larger projects Becky's students complete is a "country project" in which they select a country anywhere in the world to study. Students often work with partners on this project. After exploring information about the country in books, magazines, newspapers, CD-ROMS, and the Internet, the partners create both a portfolio and a multi-media presentation related to the people, government, and culture in their chosen country. For example, Melissa and her group created a portfolio that included information on different aspects of Chinese culture (see Figure 2-8). Another group, studying Japan, created a travel brochure as part of their portfolio (see Figure 2-9).

Becky finds that asking students to use both Internet and more traditional information sources enhances both content knowledge and research skills. As explained earlier, she sometimes facilitates sharing of the computers by setting up a station arrangement, with different resources on different computers. In addition, with partner or small group arrangements, students can split up tasks in a variety of ways. Becky explains one scenario: "When some kids are on the computers doing research or actually putting together a multimedia presentation, other kids can be working on the portfolio at their desks."

Assessment of group or partner projects can be a dilemma for teachers if they are unsure how much each student has contributed. Becky has developed a system in which students put their own names at the bottom of whatever they completed, before it is included into the group portfolio. At the end of the project, she also has students complete a form in which they evaluate their own and their group members' participation in the project. Becky also notes that she regularly assesses students through observational notes she makes while "walking around the room on a daily basis" so she could "pretty well tell who was putting forth effort and who was maybe trying to slide a little bit."

FIGURE 2-8   Essay Created as Part of a Group Portfolio Related to China

Music
By: Melissa

There is a lot of difference in Chinese music and Western music because is uses a different scale. The Western music scale uses eight tones, but the Chinese scale has five tones. The melody is an important element in Chinese music. Rather than blending in harmony, the music follows the same melodic line.

Chinese instruments are different than Western instruments also. Chinese instruments contain the qin, which is a seven-stringed instrument, the sheng, a mouth organ made of seven bamboo pipes, and a lutelike instrument called pipa. There are two kinds of flutes, the xiao and the di.

Today Chinese perform music of numerous great European composers, and they play Western instruments and music.

FIGURE 2-9 A Student-Created Tri-fold Travel Brochure About Japan

Another issue that often comes up in projects is student procrastination. Since the country project lasts about 4 weeks, Becky has learned to break the project into specific tasks that are due on specific dates. For example, a page of students' multimedia slideshow including a physical map, a political map, and a flag of the selected country with a description of the flag was often due on one date, with 2 to 3 other slides that were going into that multimedia slide show due on a later date.

WORKING AND GROWING AS A PROFESSIONAL

As the years go by, Becky finds that she needs continuous professional development, both to gain new teaching ideas and to make connections with other educators within and beyond her own community. She has used a variety of avenues for her own professional development. For example, her interest in classroom technology

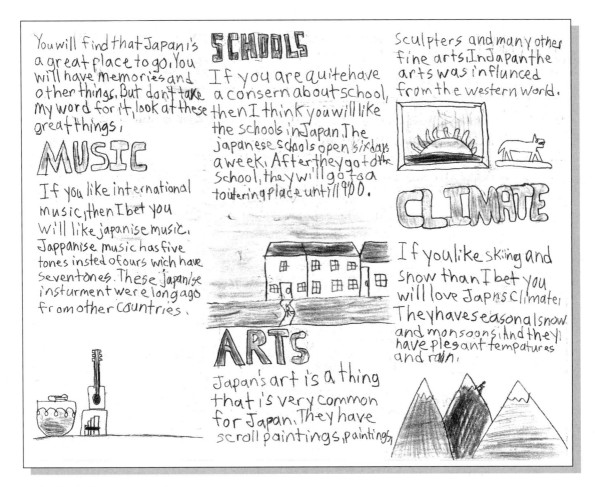

You will find that Japani's a great place to go. You will have memories and other things. But don't take my word for it, look at these great things;

MUSIC

If you like international music, then I bet you will like japanise music. Jappanise music has five tones insted of ours wich have seven tones. These japanise insturment were long ago from other countries.

SCHOOLS

If you are quite have a consern about school, then I think you will like the schools in Japan. The japanese schools open six days a week. After they got the school, they will go to a toutering place untill 900.

ARTS

Japan's art is a thing that is very common for Japan. They have scroll paintings, paintings,

Sculpters and many other fine arts. In Japan the arts was influnced from the western world.

CLIMATE

If you like skiing and snow than I bet you will love Japns climate. They have seasonal snow and monsoons. And they have plesant tempatures and rain.

FIGURE 2-9 Continued

began as a personal interest in computers, and later expanded to her classroom with the encouragement of a mentor at her school. Becky explains:

> I had always been interested in computers as a hobby. I bought one for my home and played around with it, and the more I played around with it the more I liked it and realized what a valuable tool that it could be in the classroom. So, not too much later, our district hired a technology specialist, and I took several classes and kept working at it.

The school technology specialist later encouraged Becky to apply for a grant. Becky, who was then in the first few years of her teaching career, notes that at first she was reluctant, because she "knew nothing about writing a grant . . . and had never done anything like that before." She also candidly explained that she had been concerned that actually getting the grant might cause a problem: "What if I got it? I didn't know if I'd know what to do or know how to handle it." Becky ended up applying just before the deadline and was later surprised to learn she had been selected to receive classroom computers and software.

Another avenue Becky uses for professional development is her interactions with others, including teachers, students, parents, and faculty at the nearby state university. She often reaches out into the community to locate guest speakers for her students, and ends up modifying her instruction based on new information they bring in. Becky also enjoys reading and traveling to learn about other cultures. This constant updating of her knowledge in her content area is particularly important for her world studies curriculum, as world situations change quickly and materials must be constantly evaluated for accuracy and currency.

After teaching a few years, Becky's professional interests also expanded to include working with university students in a teacher education program. She was invited to serve as the lead mentor teacher in her building for the field-based teacher education program at Texas A&M–Commerce, working with about 3 students per year. Becky has found that this role gives her the opportunity to help shape the experiences of individuals who are about to enter the field of teaching. Interestingly, she also believes that working with preservice teachers contributes to her own growth as a teacher because they bring in fresh ideas and encourage her to think more reflectively about her work.

CONCERNS

When asked what concerns she has related to her teaching, Becky spoke particularly of her interest in her students' character development, and relationships between character, self-discipline, and lifelong achievement. With the support of her principal, Becky includes materials designed to provide children information for a framework for making good decisions in their lives. Often these are personal stories about historical figures who have made positive decisions in the face of adversity or readings from inspirational books such as *Chicken Soup for the Soul* (Canfield & Hansen, 1993). Becky also has included role-playing in her lessons, in part to help students gain a deeper understanding of "the situations of our ancestors" and to look on past achievements as models for the future.

Becky also has taken a strong interest in students beyond the classroom. One major effort was the school's student council, which she helped to establish in her first years at her school. Becky says her goal was to "give the students an opportunity to participate in something in which they could feel school pride and a sense of accomplishment." The student council has had a wide variety of activities, including fund-raisers for Toys for Tots and other charitable groups. These programs have been very successful and have led to recognition for Becky and the student council members by the mayor.

Becky also is very concerned about the effects of standardized testing. In Texas, "standards based" assessments are required for all students. Students must achieve at a certain level on these tests in order to graduate. Although Becky believes that assessment is important to ensure that students are learning what they need to be learning, she worries about the tendency of teachers to "teach to the test." Becky believes the quality of instruction can be harmed when teachers begin to focus on meeting test scores, rather than providing meaningful class-room experiences.

Becky also is concerned by a lack of respect for teachers that is sometimes evident in and beyond her community. She is worried that teachers are not "respected enough as professionals." Becky believes that open communication between teachers, parents, and administrators can help to solve this problem.

▰▰ SUMMING UP ▰▰▰▰▰▰▰▰▰▰▰

Becky is a teacher who enjoys working with students both in and outside of the class-room. She is concerned about her students as individuals, taking an interest in both content learning and character development. Becky notes that she wants young people to leave her class "appreciating themselves and others" and holding a "passion for learning about our past and the thinking skills to find the answers to their questions." She also wants students to have the ability and desire to be responsible citizens. She understands her young adolescents and tries to meet them where they are, while giving them the tools and desire to move forward as citizens and learners.

- After reading this chapter, consider the following questions.
    1. What did you find most interesting or surprising when reading this case?
    2. Look back at your answers to the Thought Questions at the beginning of the chapter. How do you think that Becky describes the rewards and challenges of teaching sixth grade social studies? How is her description similar to or different from yours?
    3. In your own teaching situation, or one with which you are familiar, would it be possible to teach this way? Why or why not?
    4. Becky included a variety of types of reading, writing, and oral communication strategies in her instruction. If she wanted to increase her use of literacy even further, what else would you recommend to her?
    5. If you used the INSERT Strategy, share your marks and comments with someone in your class or study group. What are the similarities and differences?

- You may wish to use a content area literacy strategy to reflect on this case study. We suggest creating a Semantic Map (see description in Handbook, p. 146).

chapter 3

The S. S. Toy Company Project: Grade Seven

GUIDELINES

Thought Questions Consider the following questions and note your answers in a log or journal.

1. What connections do you make when you hear the words "interdisciplinary instruction"?
2. What do you see as major rewards or challenges of interdisciplinary instruction when teaching?

- Before reading, you may want to engage in a content area literacy strategy. We suggest *Prediction or PreP* (see descriptions in the Content Area Handbook, p. 143). These strategies help readers activate prior knowledge about concepts before reading.
- While reading this chapter, you may wish to use the *Save The Last Word For Me Strategy*, discussed in the Handbook (p. 145). This strategy is designed to enhance text understanding, foster group interaction, and encourage purposeful note taking. To help you determine the three most important quotes in this case, you may wish to continue using the *INSERT Strategy* (p. 138) while reading the entire chapter before creating your notecards to help you determine what is most important.
- National Standards in Interdisciplinary Instruction for Visual Arts, Technology Education, and Social Studies can be found in the Handbook and at:
  Visual Arts: www.getty.edu/artsednet/resources/scope/standards
  Technology Education: http://cnets.iste.org/sfors.htm
  Social Studies: http://peabody.vanderbilt/edu/depts/tandl/faculty/
  Myers/standards/html

The seventh grade hallways were buzzing with activity early one January. "Workers" were carrying partially completed wooden ducks from Kris's technology education wood shop where they had been cut, sanded, and assembled, to Maureen's (Mo's) art room, where they would be painted and glazed. Other workers were carrying freshly painted ducks back to the wood shop for further finishing. Student "supervisors," carrying clipboards, were tracking the production of the ducks as well as the quilted stuffed toys that were being created in the art room. A wall poster, entitled "S. S. Toy Company" listed the number of each toy that had been completed to date, in preparation for final packing before shipping to Toys for Tots (Figure 3-1).

These activities were part of an interdisciplinary project at Sandbridge Middle School that blended instruction in social studies, art, and technology education. Over a six-week period, seventh graders learned concepts related to the industrial revolution and toy design principles. They then were immersed in a 5-day simulation of a 19th century assembly line. Along the way, they used a wide variety of oral and written communication processes.

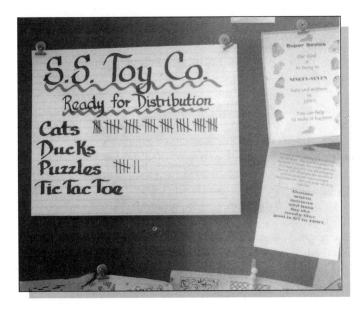

FIGURE 3-1 S.S. Toy Company Distribution List

Every seventh grade student at Sandbridge participated in the simulation, including those in the Special Education and ESOL (English for Speakers of Other Languages) programs. The school follows an inclusion model, in which special education students are mainstreamed into social studies classes and receive extra assistance from resource teachers such as Julie. Students who participate in ESOL classes study social studies with the ESOL teacher, Bonnie. All of the teachers worked collaboratively over several months to plan the simulation and orchestrate participation by over two hundred students.

BACKGROUND

Sandbridge Middle School is located in an urban area of Virginia just across the Potomac River from Washington, D. C. The school is surrounded by an older, wooded neighborhood of small brick homes, apartments, and community businesses. Parents and community members work for a wide variety of small and large corporations, governmental agencies, and the military.

About 725 students attend Sandbridge in grades 6–8. The student population is diverse and includes a growing number of students who have emigrated from countries around the world and speak a variety of home languages. Approximately 65% of the student population are of European or Middle Eastern origin, 20% are Latin American, 8% are African American, and 7% are Asian American. More than a third of the students speak a home language other than English.

Over the years, the faculty and administrators at Sandbridge have worked to develop a middle school curriculum designed to meet the needs of the school's diverse learners. Sandbridge's mission statement emphasizes a "student-centered" philosophy with a focus on high expectations for all students as well as a positive climate for learning. Student service to the community is also emphasized, with the intention that students will gain "the values necessary to become contributing members of the community." The school's website describes a wide variety of types of service that Sandbridge students perform for the community, such as collecting books, food, hats, and gloves for people in need; adopting families; visiting retirement homes; and reading to children at child-care facilities.

Another emphasis at Sandbridge is faculty collaboration. Each grade level is divided into two or three teams of "core subject" teachers who work with the same group of approximately 100 students throughout the school year. The core subject teachers include those in language arts, social studies, mathematics, and science. Teachers of health/physical education and electives such as art, music, and technology education serve several teams or grade levels but often meet with the core teams for planning. Sandbridge's principal notes that teachers at Sandbridge have substantial responsibility for developing and planning curriculum, and can modify class schedules as needed within a large block of time devoted to core class instruction each day.

Seventh Grade Collaboration

The seventh grade teachers at Sandbridge collaborate frequently on a variety of innovative projects and often create social studies "simulations" to expand their students' understanding of social studies themes. Simulations are learning experiences in which students take on roles over the course of one or more days that enable them to gain a more personalized understanding of a particular time period, culture, or occupation (Greenblat, 1988). Simulations are different than plays because scripts are not written in advance; rather, students study time periods or situations and then are immersed in a life-like situation that resembles or "simulates" historical or social conditions.

Over several years, the seventh grade teachers at Sandbridge have designed a variety of whole-team simulations that correspond to their curriculum. These have included a "Cookie Corporation" that is part of a unit on corporate structure and profits, as well as simulations on the United States Civil War and the immigrant experience on Ellis Island. The teachers have noticed that students become highly engaged in learning through these simulations and develop a more positive attitude toward social studies content and school in general. In addition, teachers find that the students improve their abstract reasoning abilities as well as their written and oral communication through participation in role-playing situations and subsequent written and oral reflections.

THE S.S. TOY COMPANY

First Steps

Kris, Sandbridge's technology education teacher, and Mo, the art teacher, first developed the idea for the "S.S. Toy Company" project, which was a simulation involving technology education, art, and the historical study of the industrial revolution. (S.S. stands for "Sandbridge Seventh.") Kris and Mo are both experienced teachers; Kris had been teaching for six years and Mo had been teaching for 20 years at the time the project began.

Kris and Mo said that one motivation for their involvement was a desire to give students who did not have space in their schedules for art or technology education a chance to experience curriculum in these areas. They also were interested in connecting the electives they taught to content area instruction and creating a service-learning opportunity for students.

During regular meetings with the content area teachers from the two seventh grade teams in early fall, Kris and Mo learned that social studies teachers Cathy and Patricia were interested in developing a simulation connected to their unit on the Industrial Revolution. Through several additional meetings that included Cathy, Patricia, Mo, and Kris as well as the special education and ESOL social studies teachers, the outline for the project as well as a time schedule emerged.

In Process

In early December, the social studies classes began their units on the Industrial Revolution. Cathy and Patricia, teachers of the American Studies classes, noted that they linked units on industrialization and immigration to the project. Reading, writing, and class discussion centered around the industrialization in the United States in the late 1800s, including the growth of the big cities, the growing population, and the use of technology and inventions. ESOL teacher Bonnie addressed similar content with her students, who read about Henry Ford and the impact of the assembly line

on automobile production. Study in all social studies classes also included the significance of the immigrants' contribution to industrialization in America.

In the art room, Mo emphasized colors and color relationships, design principles, and safety procedures in preparation for the assembly line. Kris taught students to use a variety of wood shop tools as well as computer spreadsheet and design programs.

Kris and Mo also worked behind the scenes to prepare for the simulation, which was scheduled for early January. Together they led a student planning committee that selected the toys that would be produced. This committee also distributed and collected cards on which every student listed his or her first three choices of assembly line job. The committee then developed a work schedule that included all 200 students. Kris noted that students generally received their first or second job choice, but were reminded that workers in the late 19th century generally had little choice of assembly line jobs. There also was a student "design committee" that developed the designs for the wooden ducks and the stuffed toys.

The teachers ordered materials and created samples with students in their elective courses. They also recruited these students as "supervisors" and assistant instructors to help students who did not take art and technology learn to use the technical equipment and processes.

The Simulation Experience

The assembly line began right after the winter break, on the second Monday in January. Over a five-day period, all seventh graders participated for one day. They followed a modified schedule of core classes on the other days. When on the assembly line, each student was assigned to a particular job in either the art room or the wood shop.

Students in the art room sat in assigned places at tables and did an assigned job. Art room tasks included sewing, stuffing, embroidering, and quilting for the stuffed toys, and painting and glazing for the wooden ducks. Since it was an assembly line, the tasks were divided so that each student worked on a specific object for only a short period, to complete one task. For example, some students only stuffed the toys, while others only did quilting. The toys were moved systematically down the table until they were completed. Student "supervisors" checked for quality and sent items back to individual workers if there was a task that was not completed up to standard.

In the wood shop down the hall, students all wore goggles, and received safety instructions and directions in using the equipment from Kris. Student "supervisors" followed up by assisting workers with tasks that were new to them. Wood shop tasks included cutting out wooden ducks, drilling holes, and sanding. Brian, a student, explained the process in his journal:

> There were fifteen students broken down into five working groups. The first group cut two blocks out of wood. The second group drilled holes into both blocks of wood. The third group cut one of the blocks into the shape of a duck. The fourth group sanded the wood and the fifth group screwed the wheels on the toy. My job, along with Jorge, was to drill the wood.

Pablo, another student, described the atmosphere in an essay:

> The supervisor and his pack of eighth grade thugs paced around the shop looking over the shoulders of each worker and making sure everything was running smoothly. Their rules and regulations were harsh. No talking, no procrastination, and no fooling around with the equipment!

In both the art room and the wood shop, student supervisors used check sheets on clipboards to record how many toys were created each hour. The supervisors

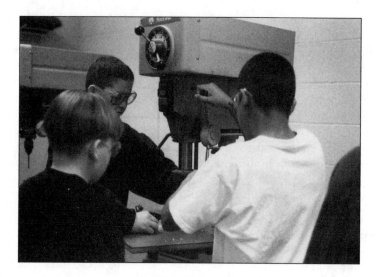

also tried to manage problems, such as those related to differences in the time required to complete each job. Mike, a student supervisor, later described one of these problems:

> I noticed that there was a slow production rate. My job was glazer, so it was up to the painters to finish their product and give it to me. Since the painters were dependent on the wood shipments they did not have a lot to paint. There weren't a lot of shipments because it took a long time to cut the wood. Even though there were setbacks I had a fun time.

At the end of each day, the teachers and student supervisors counted how many toys of each type were finished and logged them on a tally sheet (see spreadsheet in

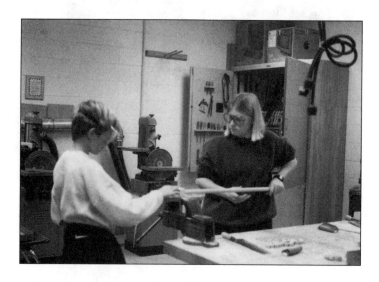

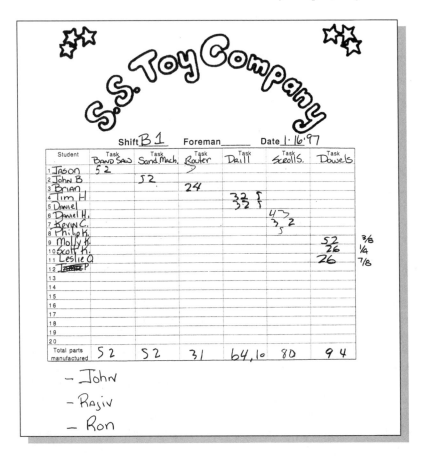

FIGURE 3-2 Spreadsheet Indicating Work of Students in the Wood Shop

Figure 3-2). At the end of the week, the student planning committee was responsible for packing all the toys and helping the teachers distribute them to community agencies.

Student Reflections

After their experience as workers on the S. S. Toy Company assembly line, students wrote several types of reflections in their social studies classes. Some students wrote from the perspective of individuals they imagined lived in the 19th century. Others described different aspects of the simulation experience. Overall, the writing assignments enabled students to link their experience in the simulation with their learning in class in a variety of ways.

Two students who wrote from the perspective of 19th century workers were Sandy and Tom. Both reflected on hardships they imagined workers of the time period might have felt. Sandy pretended to be a factory worker, writing:

My hands feel as if they are worked to the bone. My eyes are beginning to hurt because of the strain due to poor lighting. My supervisor, Mr. Radowski, was once an immigrant himself. I do not know why he beats us so hard, as he was once in our shoes.

Similarly, Tom imagined despair:

Everyday, to wake up at the crack of dawn, head over to the crowded workhouse. Deadly conditions if you ask me. My only friend at the factory passed away a couple of weeks ago. The cause was too much inhalation of sawdust. The land of opportunity, sure. For all the rich people. Not for me. I'm just stuck down here in the stupid assembly line. As long as I live, till the day I die.

Several students who wrote about the simulation experience reflected on their own motivation and learning. Juanita wrote, "My experience on the assembly line was really exciting . . . it makes you want to work on something and you know you have to get it done so the next person can do their job."

Ilene used her personal knowledge of sewing, learned at home, to evaluate a problem experienced on the assembly line: "[Quilting] wasn't hard for me because I always sew at home. [But] it was taking a long time [because] the fabric was thick and the needles weren't thin—it's easier to sew on thick fabric with big thin needles."

Other students, reflecting back to what they had learned in social studies class, demonstrated that they realized the simulation assembly line was different than an actual workplace assembly line. Elaine said that she imagined that in a real assembly line, workers would "not be allowed to talk at all" or get any help for injuries. Steven, thinking about more general factory conditions, noted, "It didn't seem real . . . there were no layoffs, speedups, or promotions."

Other students summed up how the experience helped them move beyond their classroom learning. Paul commented that "The poor working conditions and cruelty put upon immigrant factory workers have always been discussed in class, but until now, I wasn't able to understand with such clarity and sympathy. . . ." Lauren summed up her feelings about conditions for assembly line workers in the 19th century:

In the small time that I spent stuffing cats, I learned how bad the assembly line people really had it. Doing one job over and over can get really boring after awhile, but that was the least of the workers' worries. They had a small amount of breathable clean air, poor safety conditions, and a terrible climate, with barely any light. . . . I don't think any person, no matter how poor, should have to go through that just to barely get by.

Teachers' Reflections

In the follow-up interviews conducted with teachers, all indicated that they thought the simulation was a great success. Cathy, an experienced American Studies teacher, emphasized that the simulation helped her students gain a more "in depth understanding" of history as well as an "appreciation and respect for those who toil on an assembly line." Patricia, who was in her first year of teaching American Studies, agreed, adding that she found that her students "remember these types of activities and are able to compare them to what they have examined in primary and secondary sources."

Julie, who taught Special Education students in a resource setting, emphasized that her students participated in all aspects of the project as they are fully mainstreamed into the social studies classes. She said that they really enjoyed building, assembling, and packing the products they made, and benefited from the chance to connect this "hands on" learning experience to their classroom learning. Julie also noted that this project gave several of her students the chance to play managerial roles and demonstrate leadership abilities in the inclusion classroom.

Mo, the art teacher, indicated that a major benefit of the project was that the students learned to work cooperatively, improve their craftsmanship, and "use their talents to help each other." She also noted that the project required a shift in thinking for art students, who generally take their creations home. Mo said students responded very well to the requirement that these projects were created to give to others. Kris emphasized this aspect of the project as well, emphasizing that the assembly line not only helped teach content but also gave students an opportunity to help children in need.

Teachers were also asked about difficulties they encountered, and whether they would want to tackle this project or other simulations again. All resoundingly agreed that they would like to use this simulation and other simulations again. They saw any difficulties as opportunities to make changes for the future. For example, several teachers mentioned the January timing as problematic because of weather interference (several days were called off for snow), and end of semester conflicts. Cathy mentioned that the team had already decided to have the S. S. Toy Company simulation in November of the following year.

Other difficulties included the enormity of planning and scheduling for 200 students, especially since some assembly line tasks took longer than others. Students also had to learn to work carefully to create high quality toys, as the time pressure of the assembly line caused a tendency to increase speed and sacrifice quality.

Mo and Kris also had to make alternate arrangements for the 8th grade students who were normally scheduled into art and technology electives during the time period in which the simulation was held. In many cases, these students were asked to assist with teaching the younger students to use equipment and materials in the classrooms.

Sandbridge teachers also believed that this interdisciplinary project enhanced their own professional growth. Cathy mentioned that she used this and other simulations for reflective analyses in her master's program. Patricia noted that she grows as a teacher each time her students do a simulation as she can see "what works and what doesn't work" and improve her teaching for the next group. Julie said that the growth for her came from "working with a team of teachers who are creative and constantly working to include all students." Bonnie mentioned that the project gave her the chance to observe her ESOL students in a new setting and get a fresh perspective on their strengths and needs. Mo said that she learned that the students exceeded her expectations when working on the project in terms of their "effort, enthusiasm and production." Kris mentioned that he felt working with other teachers on his team and on a core team was fun and also improved his knowledge as a teacher.

FIGURE 3-3   The Finished Product

◼◼◼   SUMMING UP   ◼◼◼◼◼◼◼◼◼◼◼◼◼◼

The teachers at Sandbridge Middle School put enormous time and effort into their interdisciplinary projects, but they are pleased with the results. They find that these projects enable them to link content with hands-on learning, provide service opportunities for their students, and include every learner in a substantive way.

Throughout the project, students also developed their literacy skills through reading, writing, and discussion in social studies classes and the related use of computers, spreadsheets, and other tools in the art and technology classrooms. Throughout the project, literacy was imbedded authentically into the real work of the assembly line. Supervisors used charts to record work completion. Planners used computer spreadsheets to assist with planning the entire project. Oral communication was continually necessary among students who were taking on worker roles, and included students from various classes who may not have normally interacted in the course of their day.

Cathy summarized the feelings of the teachers by saying, "Our seventh grade team is committed to interdisciplinary projects. . . we especially like the assembly line because we were able to involve our elective teachers." Brian's comments reflected the seventh grade view: "This assembly line experience helped me to learn a lot about what it must be like to work in a factory. I also had a lot of fun."

- After reading this chapter, consider the following questions.

  1. What did you find most interesting or surprising when reading this case?

  2. Look back at your answers to the Thought Questions at the beginning of the chapter. How do you think the team describes the rewards and challenges of interdisciplinary instruction integration? How is their description similar to or different from yours?

  3. In your own teaching situation, or one with which you are familiar, would it be possible to teach this way? Why or why not?

  4. The team included a variety of types of reading, writing, and oral communication strategies in their instruction. If they wanted to increase their use of literacy even further, what else would you recommend to them?

  5. If you used the *INSERT Strategy*, share your marks and comments with someone in your class or study group. What are the similarities and differences?

- You may wish to use a content area literacy strategy to reflect on this case study. We suggest using the note cards developed while using the *Save The Last Word For Me Strategy* for discussion (see the description in the Handbook, p. 145).

chapter 4

Integrated Civics and English: Grade Eight

GUIDELINES

Thought Questions   Consider the following questions and note your answers in a log or journal.

1. What connections do you make when you hear the term "team teaching"?
2. What do you see as major advantages or disadvantages of team teaching?

- Before reading, you may want to engage in a content area literacy strategy. We suggest the *K–W–L Strategy* (see description in the Content Area Handbook, p. 139). This strategy helps readers identify what they know, what they want to find out, and what they learned from a text.
- While reading this chapter, you may wish to review the *Semantic Mapping Strategy* discussed in the Handbook, p. 146. This strategy helps readers graphically organize vocabulary to gain an understanding of larger concepts.
- National Standards in Social Studies and English/Language Arts can be found at:

  http://peabody.vanderbilt.edu/depts/tandl/faculty/Myers/standards.html

---

Visitors entering Gene and Millie's eighth grade English/Civics classroom often find it difficult to locate the teachers. On many days, their combined class of 50–60 young adolescents buzzes with somewhat noisy but productive small group activity. Millie and Gene move from group to group, asking and answering questions and probing student understanding. Along the way, they continuously observe student learning and interactions, gaining insights for future instruction. Students remain in Gene and Millie's large classroom for a double period, or a block of about ninety minutes each day. During this time, they are immersed in a highly integrated, language-rich curriculum.

Millie and Gene teach at Liberty Middle School in a suburban community located about 20 miles from Washington, D. C. Liberty serves as a neighborhood school for a diverse local population. The school also houses several magnet programs, including a Gifted and Talented (GT) program that brings together students from several middle schools. All of Gene and Millie's students are participants in the GT program.

Like many middle schools, Liberty operates on a team concept, in which approximately 100 students share the same English, social studies, math, and science teachers. These core teachers meet several times a week to discuss students' needs, curriculum, and other team issues. Millie and Gene have worked together on the same team for 5 years. However, three years ago, they took a decisive step that changed their teaching in dramatic ways. In addition to team *planning* with the other teachers on their team, Gene and Millie decided to try team *teaching* in Civics and English. Millie and Gene's classrooms are adjacent and always had been separated by a folding floor-to-ceiling partition. The year they began team teaching, the teachers worked during the summer to arrange student schedules so each student on the team would have English/Civics for a two period (90 minute) block. Then, on the first day of school, they opened the wall.

Since that time, Gene and Millie have developed a unique curriculum that merges Civics and English. The theme of their district's 8th grade Civics curriculum is *A Citizen's Journey*, which is designed to encourage students to become active members of their communities. In Millie and Gene's classes, students are engaged in a constantly evolving array of projects and activities that take them on explorations related to this theme, both within and beyond their school. They also are involved in intensive classroom work to refine and improve their knowledge and skills in civics, literature, and uses of language. In the process, they interact not only with one another and their teachers, but also with parents, university interns who work in the class for a semester, and the larger community. In this chapter we introduce Millie and Gene and provide a curriculum portrait, or overview of the types of projects, activities, and strategies they have developed. We also will take an in-depth look at an instructional unit and provide a sampling of Millie and Gene's conversations about their work and lives as teachers.

MEETING MILLIE AND GENE

Both Millie and Gene are highly experienced teachers who have taught at the middle and high school levels for over 20 years. Millie began teaching in the 1960s and has taught in several schools in the United States and in the American School in Delhi, India. Gene, who began teaching in the 1970s, has worked in several different schools in her current district. Both teachers took time off from teaching when their children were young, and they agree that this experience contributed to their skill as teachers by helping them more fully understand child development.

Although they only developed their current team approach within the last three years, Gene and Millie attribute their interest in innovative teaching to much earlier points in their lives. Millie remembers gaining an interest in teaching and also a wide knowledge of the types of teaching possible through her own experiences as a child and teenager when she attended the laboratory school of the College of Southern Mississippi (now the University of Southern Mississippi). Millie recalls that this school was developed in the 1930s according to principles of John Dewey, a leader of the progressive movement. She remembers experiencing a very hands-on curriculum when she attended in the 1940s and 50s. For example, children made dollhouse floor plans and then built the houses to scale (for mathematics), designed and made stained glass windows (for art and history), and acted out scenes from literature (for language arts). Millie remained in this school through grade 11 and later returned as a student teacher during her senior year of college. By this time she had decided to major in English, partly because she found her English professors the most interesting on the college faculty.

Gene, who attended Duke University in the 1960s, explains that as a college student she never intended to become a teacher. Gene's mother was a teacher and Gene found that from watching her mother she learned what was involved in teaching if you were going to do it the right way. However, after Gene earned her bachelor's degree in history, her mother urged her to go on immediately for a master's degree, suggesting a program at Vanderbilt University that included a teaching internship in Fairfax County, Virginia. This program was unlike traditional student teaching because Gene was expected to teach mostly on her own, without the daily support of a cooperating teacher. She believes that while it might have been nice to have someone to bounce ideas off of as a new teacher, the situation helped her learn to be flexible and take some chances. While doing her internship, Gene decided to remain in teaching, saying, "I stayed with it because I enjoyed it." During the 1970s, Gene worked in both regular and alternative high school programs. The alternative school required extensive teaming. Gene believes this early positive experience affected her recent decision to team-teach with Millie.

Looking back, Gene also recalls that as a young undergraduate she was asked to teach adult literacy classes and had to learn about teaching quickly. She believes that this experience helped her learn to individualize instruction because the adult students were at different stages of learning and their class attendance was irregular. Gene succinctly explains: "I developed the recognition, when I was 18 or 19 years old, that I had to make allowances for all of the [students'] differences. I didn't learn that out of a book . . . I learned that on the beat."

INSIDE MILLIE AND GENE'S CLASSROOM

Gene and Millie think that classroom organization is important, especially in a team-teaching situation. A visitor walking into their double room will see the teachers' desks in the far left and right corners. The back wall is a maze of file cabinets, shelves crammed with books, boxes of student portfolios, poster board, art supplies, and other materials. Blackboards, posters explaining the grading system, and student work cover the walls to the side and the front of the room. Several easels with chart paper and an overhead projector also are used frequently.

Approximately 55 student desks are spread throughout the center of the large room, often in different arrangements on different days. When planning their management strategies, Gene and Millie decided to put a permanent number on each desk and assign the number to a student in each class. With this system, they can use the desk numbers to make specific group assignments. Early in the morning, they might put desks into groups of three or four, into rows, or into a large semi-circle. As students enter class throughout the day, they first must locate their own desks, then sit down and prepare to work.

Beginning the Year

Millie and Gene have developed specific activities that they use in the beginning of the year to learn more about their students' individual interests, strengths, and needs. They also use strategies to help students transition from previous non-teamed situations to the team-teaching setting. For example, the teachers say that they have found it helpful to keep their movable wall open during the first days of the school year in order to give students the sense that they are in a two-period block. After the two groups of students have become used to the idea that they are really all one class, Gene and Millie move them in and out of different groupings depending on the day's activity. The teachers say that one important reason they use group work at this point in the year is to observe students' interactions, interests, and talents. As the year progresses, this information helps Gene and Millie build a curriculum that serves students' needs.

Millie and Gene also think it is vital to develop a sense of community within their classroom, and they connect this to their curricular study of community. As Gene explains:

> The community [concept] gives us an opportunity to address the different elements that you have to have within a community . . . so we define a model community. And then we talk about modeling and the fact that we use models in the social sciences . . . and we use school as a model . . . [helping students see that] we are all here with a common interest, but . . . we have rights and responsibilities.

During the first week of school, the teachers include their school district's statement of Students' Rights and Responsibilities as material for reading and discussion. All middle school students are required to study this document, and it logically fits into the curriculum at this point. In addition, by using this document as part of the curriculum, Gene and Millie make the point early on that Civics is part of everyday life, and not just a school subject.

Making Connections

In describing how she and Millie develop their joint curriculum, Gene points out that "lots of things . . . can fit into that blanket [the study of community]." One overriding goal of the teachers is to help students see the big picture—or how concepts relate to one another.

As the year continues, each area of study grows logically from the one before it. For example, Gene finds that one spin-off or topic related to the study of community is the evolution of government. Within this theme, the classes consider how and why communities create governments. Related literature is included—for example, Millie has found that the books *Animal Farm* (Orwell, 1946) and *Lord of the Flies* (Golding, 1954) fit well at this point and help students understand difficult civics concepts. While reading the novels, students write essays about issues related to community and government and discuss their responses in small groups. They also consider personal meanings of community by identifying their own communities; they then communicate this information about themselves in essays and graphic designs. Students use the designs to decorate their Social Studies/English writing folders (see Figure 4-1). The personal designs also are discussed with their teachers and with others in the class, which serves to increase understanding and builds a sense of community within each class.

Millie also has instituted a program of individualized reading, which students complete throughout the year. Although most of their students read well, the teachers have found that some students choose to read very little on their own. Millie explained her thinking in deciding how to structure the program: "I sort of

FIGURE 4-1   Students' Pictorial Interpretations of Their Communities

mulled over how I was going to do it . . . and I think in eighth grade, [students] need to . . . begin to take ownership of [their reading] themselves." With this in mind, Millie decided to require that students set their own reading goals for free-choice reading. She reviews goals with each student and requires that at the end of each quarter they write reflections. Students must explain why goals were met or not met and must set goals for the following quarter. They also are occasionally asked to share their thoughts about books in a variety of ways. For example, in one assignment students wrote letters to a character in a book they had read to demonstrate an understanding of the character's personality and the time period of the book.

Moving Forward

As the year moves forward, Gene and Millie continue to use concepts related to the Civics curriculum as central themes. Students study elections, economics, and their local, state, and federal governments. Themes are explored and developed through a wide variety of inquiry activities that integrate the study of literature and English/Language Arts goals into the curriculum. Millie and Gene believe this type of curricular integration is possible partly because their district's programs of study for both 8th grade English and Civics are flexible. Civics includes the topics mentioned earlier; in addition, all 8th grade students in the district are required to complete service hours as part of the Civics curriculum. The English curriculum is process-oriented, with the expectation that students will become increasingly proficient readers, writers, and communicators. Teachers have choices of literature and other materials.

The unique program Millie and Gene have developed reflects their strong philosophical belief in multi-dimensional curriculum integration. Within the Civics course, a number of social studies disciplines are integrated. At the same time, the English/Language Arts goals are integrated with those from Social Studies in both courses. Gene explains her view on the first point: "[for example] . . . I do economics and geography together because I don't think you can do one without the other." In essence, as Gene and Millie merge their objectives, lines blur between disciplines so that school learning resembles learning outside of school.

Another major goal Gene and Millie share is to help students become inquirers who can think like social scientists and communicate effectively with a wide range of people. They involve students, parents, community members, and teacher interns from a local university in the development of projects, which vary each year. For example, classes have created historical primary-source documents through interviews with community members, made a large quilt illustrating the lives of local citizens, written a class book on the history of their community, and filmed a professional-quality video for a CNN contest on youth and elections.

For all projects, students have both individual and group assignments. The teachers believe that group work is valuable but can be overused. Groups in their classes are formed based on the requirements of a particular project, and group membership generally changes with new assignments.

Community Involvement

One hallmark of Gene and Millie's curriculum is the way in which parents and other community members are included. Gene and Millie invite a wide variety of adults to speak to classes and share their talents in other ways. In some cases, parents and other community members even help develop curriculum in areas of personal expertise. For example, during their first year of team-teaching, Gene and Millie developed a unit on the history of the town in which the school is located. They invited a parent who is an historian to teach students how to conduct and transcribe interviews with standard social science research methods. Using tape recorders, students interviewed local residents who had lived in the area for at least 15 years. As a result of the parent–historian's visits, Gene and Millie revised their original expectations and required students to adhere to interview and transcription methods used by social scientists (see Figure 4-2). At the end of the project, a local university was anxious to include the documents in their collection on local history. As Millie explains:

> [The project] really evolved primarily because we had a lot of parental help . . . this particular woman who was really an expert . . . guided us in really getting historical primary sources from these students . . . and we ended up donating those to the George Mason [University] library . . . so that was [the students'] community service project.

Interestingly, involvement of a few parents has even continued beyond one year. For example, the parent–historian who worked on the interview project returned the following year to work with the next group of 8th graders, even though her own child had gone on to high school.

Other parents or community members who have visited the class include a local delegate to the state legislature, a parent who is a member of a local activist group, the editor of a newspaper, and representatives of a cable TV station. Students also make individual and group visits—such as a small-group visit to the cable TV studio to learn videotape editing, a whole-class visit to the State Capitol in Richmond, and individual visits to interview community members.

THE VOLUNTEERISM UNIT

In the spring of their second year of team teaching, Gene and Millie developed a unit that integrated their district's 8th grade volunteer requirement into an expanded project on volunteerism. Gene explains their thinking:

> Our goals in Social Studies and one of my personal goals for the students is that they become contributing members of the communities they live in. . . . We thought that one good way for them to do that was to talk to people who had actually put themselves out on the line and given their time and their resources . . . to various aspects of the community.

This unit required students to interview community members, as previous classes had done in the Reston history project. However, the new unit had a different focus, which Gene and Millie felt was important partly because they did not want students

---

Transcription of Oral History Interview

<u>Interviewer:</u> Matthew

<u>Subject:</u> Leomia   manager of the Closet

<u>Date:</u> January 19, 1998

<u>Time:</u> 2:30 pm

<u>Place:</u> The Closet in Herndon, Virginia

<u>Question #1:</u> What caused you to be interested in this project in the first place?

<u>Answer:</u> Well, let me tell you how I got started first of all. As a member of our congregation in Reston who sponsors the Closet, each church sends two representatives to the board of directors. I was asked by one of our church members if I would work on the board and I said yes. Basically, what that involved was just going to the meetings and determining what happens to the proceeds from the sales, the money that we make here. That's how I got started. I was not an employee. I was just a volunteer. And once I got into being a volunteer, that went into being or becoming a staff member and basically the reason I like it is because it is a service organization.

<u>Question #2:</u> Do you know anything about the organization from its beginning and when it was started?

<u>Answer:</u> I do. Actually, the Closet was started in 1973. Local churches in the area got together and decided to form an organization that would be of interest to the community in terms of buying clothing at a cost that was not extremely expensive. That was the main goal at the time. That was in the spring of 1973. The Closet was started in a building

---

FIGURE 4-2   First Page of Student's Interview Transcription

to have to repeat the project of an earlier class. There also was a very practical reason for changing projects, as Millie explained matter-of-factly: "Of course . . . you can't do the same thing because [the previous classes] had already interviewed all those people [Reston residents]." This concern highlights what Gene and Millie have discovered as the need to be constantly aware of the real-life personal dimensions of projects that go beyond the boundaries of the school.

National events also influenced the teacher's decision-making, as Millie explained: "We thought of the idea of having them interview volunteers because . . . it's an issue . . . there are news articles about it . . . the President's saying everybody should do this." In addition, as Gene pointed out, the topic of volunteerism raised political issues students could explore: "There are pros and cons . . . when [the government] cuts funds, it's usually for social services, and volunteers have to pick it up, or it's lost through the cracks."

The new unit met numerous English and Social Studies curricular requirements, including the school district's community service requirement. Students would once again be contributing the results of their work to the University archives to assist future researchers. Gene commented that this aspect of their interview projects had proven very valuable to students, who seemed to work much harder when they knew their work had a real audience. In addition, the teachers saw this as an opportunity for students to do something "more meaningful and . . . maybe more lasting" than the one-day projects many had completed in the past.

Planning and Beginning

As the teachers planned the unit, they developed core requirements, including that students would select an area of personal interest and locate a volunteer who was not a family member. Students were asked to schedule the interview themselves, develop questions, conduct the interview, and transcribe it according to guidelines provided by the parent–historian. Parents of all students were informed of the project through a letter that had to be signed and returned to the teachers. Gene and Millie felt this was especially important since the interviewing and transcription work were done outside of class time.

Student Efforts

As long as they interviewed a volunteer who helped the community in some way, students had several options for this project. They chose their topics, person to interview, and interview questions. Although they were precluded from interviewing family members, students could interview people they already knew, such as coaches. Millie and Gene explained that while some took this "easy" route, other students went to great lengths to find an interviewee in a special area of interest. For example, Millie describes one student who wanted to interview a person who helped animals:

> . . . she called [many places] and didn't get answers . . . she finally ended up with a woman who takes in ferrets because people buy them for pets and then don't want them . . . she had 45 ferrets in her house.

Another student called numerous organizations, eventually arranging an interview with an extraordinary volunteer who led a wide variety of projects. Gene commented: "Probably [the student] learned more from [this volunteer] than she could have from any other thing we did during the year about being part of the community." Both teachers said they thought students often worked harder on projects such as this because they were responsible for making decisions about various aspects of the process.

Students also had the option of asking an adult to help with transcribing their audiotapes. Most completed the transcriptions themselves, although Gene and Millie said that some students complained about this tedious process. Millie said she countered these complaints by reminding students that they were creating something of lasting value because "if you don't do a transcript, you don't have a primary document." She also advocates being honest with students right from the beginning, saying the students responded well when she told them: "This is tedious, it's very time consuming, but you will be producing something that is invaluable for research."

Uses of Language

When asked about ways students used reading, writing, and other language forms during the unit, Millie responded ". . . they're just using language, the whole time." In addition to the oral communication involved in telephoning, interviewing, and subsequent group discussion, students completed several types of writing to describe and analyze their experience during the project. For example, they wrote narratives describing "the whole process that they went through to do this interview," answers to reflective questions including "How would you do this differently next time?" and descriptions of the setting where the interview took place. Millie explained that the writing required students "to synthesize the information" and "evaluate their own learning at the end." A sample of student writing is shown in Figure 4-3.

Bringing It All Together

Late in the spring after students had turned in their interviews, Gene and Millie designed several class sessions for group interaction on the project. These classes took approximately 3 of their double periods. During this time, students worked as a whole class, in small groups, and as individuals to analyze, interpret, and summarize the interviews the class had conducted.

On the first day, Gene and Millie began with each whole double class of 50 students together. The teachers asked students to think back over the volunteer project and brainstorm what they had learned about volunteers and volunteerism in their community (see *Brainstorming* in the Handbook). Gene and Millie worked in tandem, with Gene eliciting generalizations from the class, and Millie working at one side of the room creating a semantic map illustrating students' ideas (see Figure 4-4).

After this introduction, Gene and Millie gave out work packets to each small group of 4 students. Each packet contained 4 transcribed interviews that had been completed by other members of their class. Care was taken to insure that groups did not get interviews conducted by their own members. The teachers also tried to put "a variety" in each packet, in terms of level of excellence. As Millie explained: "One of the purposes in having them look through [the interviews of others] is to [help students] become aware of the differences . . . because some of the questions were a lot better than others." In addition, she believed that seeing another's work sometimes helps students become more reflective about how to improve their own work, because "without having to directly talk about that, I think indirectly they see what other kids are doing." Reading their classmates' interviews also gave students the chance to work with and appreciate the primary source documents their class created.

> ### Report of Oral History Interview
>
> Long before I had even heard about the oral history project I had met and knew the person I would interview. My family is volunteering for VEFC, which stands for Volunteer Emergency Families for Children. It is a volunteer-based program in which families provide immediate care for neglected children for a maximum of twenty-one days until new guardianship is found for the children. My family attended training courses in October at the Fairfax County Office of Social Services, and it was there I met Sherry Carrigan, who conducted the training classes. Later, when the oral history project was introduced to me, Mrs. Carrigan came to my mind as an excellent example of a person showing leadership in their community. I especially thought so when I found out that not only is Mrs. Carrigan a member of a volunteer host family, but the Program Coordinator of VEFC as well. I wrote my proposal with Mrs. Carrigan in mind and researched some more about VEFC in some information booklets my family has.
>
> Dr. Larson, after a few concerns, approved my proposal. She had wondered if Mrs. Carrigan was paid to do this. Mrs. Carrigan is paid for being Program Coordinator, but was not for her previous experience on the Advisory Board, and is not for being a volunteer host family. I had already called Mrs. Carrigan to see how she felt if I interviewed her for this project in early December. She said she would feel honored, and asked me to call her after the holidays. In the meantime I drafted questions and worked out plans of how to go about conducting the interview.
>
> On Saturday, January 3, I called Mrs. Carrigan. We set the interview for Saturday, January 10 at 11:00 a.m. I suggested my house for the interview, but she volunteered her house. Since she worked from her home office, I figured her house had to be a pretty quiet place, so I agreed. She asked me to send her a copy of my

FIGURE 4-3   Oral History Interview Sample

Group members were instructed to pass the four interviews among themselves until each person had read all of the interviews. As they read, students were expected take notes related to characteristics of the volunteers in the different interviews. Each group then worked together to make a visual display on tagboard depicting generalizations about volunteerism they made from the interviews their group had read. The teachers posted instructions for this poster, which they called "Profile of Volunteers," on the wall (see Figure 4-5).

During the small group work, Millie, Gene, and Katie (a teacher intern from a local university) circulated among students, answering questions and helping everyone stay on task. Group members could be seen reading interviews, making notes, comparing ideas with other group members, and writing these ideas on the tagboard. Many groups also used illustrations and graphic organizers in their visuals. At

FIGURE 4-4 Teachers Lead a Brainstorming Session

FIGURE 4-5 Students' "Profile of Volunteers" Visual

#1 Profile of Volunteers

Directions: Based on the interviews assigned to your group, design a graphic showing the following traits of volunteers and attitudes toward volunteering:

1. Categories represented
2. Personalities
3. Motivation
4. Personal rewards
5. Drawbacks
6. Value to community

• At the bottom add a list of "sources," the names of the people interviewed in your assigned interviews.

• You may embellish your design with any appropriate illustrations.

• Include the names of all members of your group.

the end of the ninety-minute period, two groups who were ready to share went to the front of the room and explained their visuals. Millie and Gene used this opportunity to help students summarize what they had learned in class that day.

Over the next two days, all groups finished and shared their visuals (see Figure 4-6). Groups then were asked to pull quotations from the interviews to support their generalizations and all classes combined their findings on a large summary chart that was hung in the hall. This chart was arranged in categories students developed by reading the interviews; for example, "personality traits," "motivation," and "personal rewards." As Millie explained, the whole-class chart pulled together information from the individual group charts and illustrated the wide range of characteristics and attitudes of volunteers.

SYNTHESIS AND EXTENSION

Gene and Millie have found that one positive result of their interviewing projects has been attention and response from the local community. The first year project was done as part of a community-wide celebration of the thirtieth anniversary of the town of Reston, and Gene commented that "the response from the community was tremendous . . . they were so appreciative of what the students were doing." The second year project was not focused on one town, partly because the students come from several towns. Nonetheless, Millie commented that she had been "hearing people comment about being interviewed and that the kids did a really good job." In essence, the teachers have found these projects inspire two-way learning between the community and the students, as the projects have "increased the community's appreciation of what kids can do in 8th grade" and also increased students' understanding of real-life issues in the community. Several volunteers, for example, discussed the types of savings to government that volunteerism provides with their student interviewers, which gave students an increased understanding of economics. There also were some unplanned benefits of the intergenerational contact

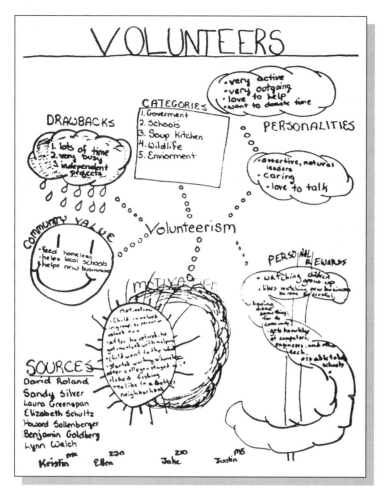

FIGURE 4-6   Students' Visual Depicting Characteristics of Volunteers

between students and community members. For example, when the project was displayed at the county fair, an older person approached one of the 8th graders and expressed tremendous gratitude for his role in helping to record local history. Millie and Gene said that these comments made a lasting impression on this particular student, as he had previously doubted the value of the project and complained about the time it took.

The teachers also were proud of students who had grown in personal ways—for example, several students who seemed to be "very shy kids" told Gene and Millie that making phone calls and going to their interview was "a very, very scary experience." Looking back, however, these students felt self-satisfaction and "knew it would be so much easier [to do something similar] in the future." Interestingly, both teachers and students found that those who had interviewed people they never met before "had the best interviews." It seems that these students asked better, more detailed questions. By contrast, one student who interviewed his coach commented that he had a hard time asking questions because he already knew so much about the interviewee.

In summary, results of the community interviewing projects have been complex. Gene, Millie, their students, and the local community have found both projects interesting and valuable. As a part of a yearlong team curriculum, these projects help students use language in a wide variety of ways while learning numerous principles of civics. They also contribute to an atmosphere that engages the attention of these 8th graders while providing service to the community.

ASSESSMENT

Gene and Millie view assessment as the continual observation of students and their learning. Students keep portfolios of their work that are reviewed by the teachers, parents, and students themselves. Some assignments, such as the independent reading project, require students to set goals and later reflect on their own progress. Students also are taught to self-assess their learning and written products.

Throughout the year, the teachers use assessments to direct their teaching. For example, when Millie notices that students have problems with particular skills, such as the use of apostrophes, she gives short, focused "mini-lessons." Later, she says she "might give a test that says 'tell me everything you know about the apostrophe and how to use it'" to help students reflect on their learning. She then expects students to apply this knowledge in future written work, while recognizing that their progress may be uneven since learning to write takes time. Millie and Gene grade writing assignments with rubrics, but only after students have had several chances to revise for content and edit their work.

While Millie and Gene do not see assessment and grading as the same, they must give grades in both Civics and English. They have developed a system for their teamed classes in which assignments are graded for Civics, English, or both. A chart posted on the wall shows students how projects and assignments count for the different subjects.

CONVERSATIONS WITH GENE AND MILLIE

Although Gene and Millie are dedicated teachers who have met with a great deal of success, they do not see teaching as either easy or problem-free. During the interviews they talked extensively about team teaching, students, challenges they have faced, and ways they stay current.

On Teaming

Millie and Gene agree that team teaching can be difficult and will not work in every situation. Why has teaming worked for them? First, the teachers *chose* to team-teach, knowing they shared similar teaching philosophies. Yet their teaching is not identical, and they both came into the situation with many years of experience "doing their own thing." Gene explains the necessary give-and-take: "[You have to be] willing . . . to *leave something out* . . . I've had to be willing NOT to do some of my 'pet' things . . . because

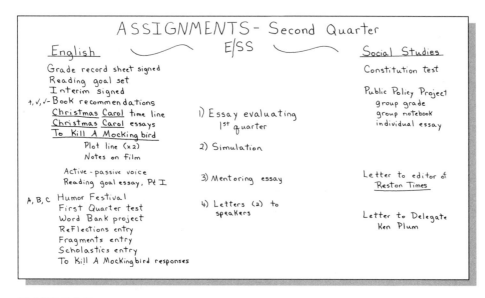

FIGURE 4-7 Chart Depicting Student Assignments

[they] really didn't work [with the teamed curriculum] . . . and I know Millie's had the same experience. There's just not enough time [to do everything]."

In addition, Millie and Gene believe that one of the most important reasons for their success in team teaching is their ability to *listen* to each other, both during planning and while the other is teaching. Each teacher usually remains in the room when the other is teaching: "One of the reasons why we've been able to work together is that we do listen to each other . . . it can't be 'turn teaching'." Their teaching is well planned, but allows flexibility for the unexpected. As an example, once when Gene invited a guest speaker to Civics class, Millie saw "an opportunity to have the kids write a thank-you letter of some substance." The speaker was a parent who discussed local zoning issues. Soon after students wrote this letter for English, Gene took the business letter format they had learned and taught them how to convert it to write a letter to the editor of the local newspaper regarding their own views on zoning. Gene emphasized that she helped students with grammar and insisted they make corrections before they mailed letters, commenting that team teachers should have consistency in their expectations and "be careful that the English teacher doesn't become the grammarian."

Another key element of Gene and Millie's success has been their openness and willingness to involve others in their instruction. In addition to numerous guest speakers, they have also welcomed teacher education interns from the Professional Development School program at George Mason University into their classroom for four years. From the first day of school, students are taught to think of the interns as a third teacher and respond well to their leadership. These interns work in the classroom for a semester, with some days spent at the university for class work. Gene comments that interns have enhanced the teaming situation: "The third person [makes it much easier] . . . particularly with the kind of children we are getting now who are used to having a lot of individual attention and giving their opinion about everything." Interns have noted that Gene and Millie give them extraordinary freedom to develop special projects. For example, one intern helped students write a book on the town's history while another led an extensive video project during a presidential election.

On Students

Since Gene and Millie's students all have been identified as academically gifted, others sometimes assume that there is no diversity within the group. The teachers say that while compared to some other classes, they find their students "a little more focused on doing the academic work," they feel it is important to remember that developmentally, the students are as varied as any group of young teenagers. Millie believes that her experience with different age groups helps her to understand how maturation and learning are connected. As she says, "I've taught grades 7 through 12, [which] gives a kind of perspective [of the students'] maturation, particularly with language development . . . because sometimes you need to wait and let them grow a year—it's a matter of just getting there, and you can't push it. . . ." Gene explains that she learned a great deal about child and adolescent development from observing her own children over time. She says, "I think [with] your own children, you see how at one stage in their lives they [might] make a tremendous leap forward . . . before having my own family, I don't think I had a sense of that."

Overall, Gene and Millie think that "kids at this age learn best if they're doing something with what they learned," because eighth graders ("even these really bright kids") "don't always see the connections" between ideas or understand abstract concepts. The teachers think an integrated curriculum that includes both "doing" and extensive use of language goes a long way toward developing students' understanding. In addition, they emphasize that teachers must take the time to be sure students are getting the "big picture." As Millie explains, "you have to continually [explain the connections] or they don't [understand] what you're doing."

An example of their communication with students is the wall poster in Figure 4-7, which shows which assignments are due for each class, and which are due for the joint (E/SS) class.

Facing Challenges

All teachers must find ways to cope with challenges present in the school environment. For example, like many teachers, Millie and Gene find lack of planning time to be a major challenge. Although they have a shared planning period, team meetings, paperwork, and a host of other necessary activities often take this time. They say they save some time by combining their storehouse of ideas and materials from past years with current material. In addition, they trust each other, their university intern, and even some guest presenters to "take charge" of different activities, which allows each person to prepare in more depth. As mentioned earlier, Gene and Millie also think communication is necessary for effective planning. As Millie says, ". . . our planning really has been by listening to each other more than anything."

Within their school, Millie and Gene have found their administration highly supportive of their team teaching. Even so, problems occasionally occur. For example, one fall they returned to school to find that accidentally, their classes had not been scheduled back-to-back. Gene and Millie, along with their university intern, spent extensive time during the first two weeks of school rescheduling all of their students so that they could continue team teaching. While they found this task somewhat overwhelming at the start of the school year, Gene and Millie worked to overcome it because of their strong belief in the value of teaming.

Recently, Gene and Millie also have had to spend extensive time insuring that their curriculum aligns with new mandates in their state, including new state "standards of learning" in every subject and a range of new competency tests. This has required a variety of adjustments, including redesign of some units of study. In working to maintain the most beneficial aspects of their innovative curriculum within the new constraints, Gene and Millie have relied heavily on their own in-depth professional knowledge and beliefs about teaching and learning.

STAYING CURRENT

Gene and Millie also work to stay current with ideas in their fields. On one hand, their years of experience have taught them that many ideas that might seem new have really been in existence for a long time. As discussed earlier, Gene recalls teaching an inquiry-based social studies curriculum in the 1970s, for example, while Millie had childhood experience with a progressive-era curriculum in the 1940s. Nonetheless, the teachers continue to value the discussion and spark that comes from sharing teaching ideas with others. Their connection with the university has been important, as they find their interns often bring fresh perspectives. The teachers also have participated in a variety of workshops and courses, such as the "clinical faculty course" both took when they began working with the university students. In addition, they continue exploration in their own fields and share related insights with their students. For example, Millie recently attended a workshop taught by William Faulkner's editor, who discussed the writing process and emphasized that even acclaimed writers often have to revise their work in order to be published. Millie says that this information has an impact on eighth grade writers, who sometimes are very reluctant to revise their own work.

Other types of professional development are less formal, but also important. For example, Millie often discusses educational issues with her sister, who is a linguist. Gene, whose mother and aunt were both teachers, has had many family discussions related to education and recently inherited a large quantity of teaching-related materials. Overall, both teachers continue to be learners, always exploring different ways of teaching that are interesting and valuable.

SUMMING UP

Gene and Millie are a team that has made a difference for hundreds of adolescents. Their knowledge about teaching and learning, built through years of experience and personal inquiry, is extensive. Through the years they also have maintained highly positive attitudes and remained open to new ideas, balancing flexibility with professional decision-making. In observing their work with eighth graders, it is clear that they really *like* teenagers and care about each student as an individual. Their curriculum and their team example challenges students to do their best, to work cooperatively, and to go beyond themselves.

- After reading this chapter, consider the following questions.
  1. What did you find most interesting or surprising when reading this case?
  2. Look back at your answers to the Thought Questions at the beginning of the chapter. How do you think that Millie and Gene describe team teaching? How is their description similar to or different from yours?
  3. In your own teaching situation, or one with which you are familiar, would it be possible to teach this way? Why or why not?
  4. Gene and Millie included a variety of types of reading, writing, and oral communication strategies in their instruction. If they wanted to increase their uses of literacy even further, what else would you recommend to them?
  5. If you completed a semantic map, compare it with someone in your class or study group. What are the similarities and differences?
  6. If you used *K–W–L*, compare what you learned with someone in your class or study group. What are the similarities and differences?

- You may wish to use a content area literacy strategy to reflect on this case study. We suggest using the *Sketch to Stretch Strategy* (see description in the Handbook, p. 153). This strategy helps readers represent the most important "picture" that plays in their minds when they read a selection.

chapter 5

High School Biology

> **GUIDELINES**
>
> **Thought Questions**   Consider the following questions. You may wish to write your ideas in your journal or discuss them with others.
>
> 1. What connections do you make when you hear the phrase "teaching biology"?
> 2. What do you see as major sources of pleasure and problems of teaching biology?
>
> - Before reading, you may want to engage in a content area literacy strategy. We suggest the *Brainstorming Strategy* (see description in the Content Area Handbook, p. 132). This strategy helps readers activate schema in order to maximize comprehension.
> - While reading this chapter, you may wish to use the *Categorization Strategy*, discussed in the Handbook (p. 132). This strategy helps readers determine hierarchical relationships.
> - National Standards in Science can be found at: www.nap.edu/readingroom/ books/nses/html/overview.html#teaching

It is seven-fifty on Monday morning. Ellen and Judy, two of the twenty-one biology students in Karen's first period Advanced Placement (AP) Biology class, rush into the classroom with a copy of *The Dallas Morning News*. Karen is preparing group materials for a lesson at the front lab table, and smiles as they enter. "Did you see the paper Mrs. S? We're on page 19A!"

Karen laughs and holds up three copies of the same newspaper. She points to the wall where she has posted a copy of page 19A with all of the science fair winners from her classes highlighted in blue. They gather around the lab table, open the newspa-

pers, and share their impressions of the 40th annual Dallas Regional Science and Engineering Fair. As other students come in, the atmosphere is relaxed and casual discussions abound as students share and discuss the newspaper story about their award-winning work. Over 100 schools were represented and 900 students in grades 7 through 12 entered projects in the regional contest. These students are proud because 23 students from their school were award winners at the science fair competition and three were grand prize winners in the senior division. These three winners were to move on to the state level competition later in the week.

And so begins a new week in Karen's biology classes in a suburban school district just north of Dallas, Texas. The school district serves approximately 40,000 students, mainly from middle- to upper-middle class backgrounds. Karen's school serves over 3,000 students and has a long history of academic excellence and innovative programs. The student population is mostly Anglo, but also includes students of Asian, African American, Hispanic, Indian, and Middle Eastern backgrounds. Over ninety-five percent attend college after high school graduation.

Karen teaches Biology II and Advanced Placement (AP) Biology II, both of which fulfill the district's third year science requirement. To enroll in Biology II or AP Biology II, students must complete Biology I and Chemistry as prerequisites. Students in Karen's classes can be juniors or seniors and most of the students who take AP Biology II do so because of a strong interest in science.

The school day is divided into seven hour-long blocks. Karen's first section of AP Biology II occurs during the first and second hours and includes 21 students. The third hour of Karen's day is for conferences and the fourth hour is for lunch. A second section of AP Biology II occurs during the fifth and sixth hours. This class is made up of fifteen girls and nine boys; several of these students immigrated to the United States during middle or high school and have only been learning English for the past few years. Karen's final class of the day, Biology II, includes 24 students.

MEETING KAREN

Karen has been teaching for 14 years, with assignments mainly in Biology and Independent Research for grades 9 through 12. Although this is her first year teaching AP junior and seniors in Biology II, she previously served as a team leader and department chair of science in a different school in the district that serves only freshmen and sophomores. Karen shifted to her new position because she wanted the challenge of preparing students to receive college credit for their work and to further her own research agenda.

When asked to reflect on her own growth as a teacher, Karen recalls that during her undergraduate work she thought "pretty much like a student" rather than a teacher, so did not get much out of her teacher preparation program. She now wishes that she had gone into more schools to observe as an undergraduate.

Karen went on to explain that when she first started teaching, she was very shy and at 22 felt she didn't know what she was doing in the classroom. Unfortunately, she team-taught with an older teacher whom she said "really ruled" how Karen behaved in the classroom. She recalls:

> I was under a misconception during those years that in team teaching you had to teach exactly the same way and do the same thing. I didn't realize that you could cover the same amount of information in a different way. The first 6 or 7 years are sort of a blur and I don't really remember what I did in there, I just felt like a robot. I know that students were not as important to me at that time because I was following a dictatorship type teacher. She was a master of what she presented but kids' work was the least of her concern.

When Karen's teammate left for another school and a remodeling project disrupted the regular way of doing things, she believes a metamorphosis occurred in her teaching. She was faced with a very difficult situation because when the school year started, there were no desks, no chairs, and no materials in the storerooms. Karen recalls:

> I was constantly saying to kids, 'Ok, tomorrow we need this for that, you all are going to get it and bring it in.' Before that year I would never have said in order to do this you need this, you need to be responsible. I was amazed at how much the kids could do and that really began to open up my eyes in terms of what I could expect of them.

When asked if she would characterize herself as a student-centered teacher, Karen nods "yes" but notes that she is in transition because this is her first year teaching the AP Biology II and Biology II courses. She says:

> I feel like a new teacher again because I have to refine and extend my knowledge of the content, adjust the teaching/learning strategies to fit the age and needs of these students, figure out what is important and/or difficult to understand, and appropriately mesh strategies with the content.

Overall, Karen has found that through her years of teaching she has had to constantly learn new things. She believes that her education as a teacher is never over and says she enjoys and tends to seek out new challenges to prevent becoming "stale" in her work.

INSIDE KAREN'S CLASSROOM

When entering Karen's classroom, visitors notice student work and science information covering the walls. These displays are related to the wide variety of assignments and projects Karen uses to reach students and meet their learning needs throughout the year. One of her main goals is to spark her students' interest in scientific questions and research. She also believes that even her advanced students still need a teacher who helps them "learn how to learn" in science.

Overall Goals

Karen says that when she first meets her students, many say they hate science. She thinks that in reality they only hate the lecture/memorization-style teaching that may have characterized their previous science instruction. She works to counter these negative feelings by immersing students in activities that reflect the everyday lives of practicing scientists. Exploration of science concepts is linked to students' own questions about science, and classroom practices include experimentation, reading background data on concepts explored, and communicating science learning through writing (such as lab reports) and discussion with others.

Karen also works to expose her students to real world applications so they gain a deeper appreciation for the importance of studying science concepts. From the first day of class, she tells students that "biology is everywhere" and models her own fascination with the study of life. Karen says she is always on the lookout for materials that will catch student interest. For example, she showed a David Attenborough timelapse video of plant growth that showed plants killing other life forms. Class discussion was animated and students spontaneously shared their previous knowledge on comparative growth speeds of various life forms.

Awareness of Student Needs

In addition to thinking about ways to help students learn science, Karen considers her students' needs as individuals, both in and beyond the classroom. She says that education should be "student centered" so that teachers maintain a balance between the best interests of the students and clear curricular goals. Karen explains:

> I really believe in the kids; [I] try to monitor and work with the kids. Sometimes I know that Biology is not really important for a student that day; they just have their things going on and we need to deal with them.

A simple yet effective technique Karen uses to stay in touch with students' needs is to stand in the classroom doorway and watch and listen as they enter the classroom each day. Karen explains,

> I want to know what kind of day they are having. I hate it when I get there after they do because I really don't know what's going on with them. I can tell more when they walk in the door than any other time during the class.

Karen gives an example of a senior who wanted to talk about universities when he came into class. As she got the lesson underway and got the class going on group work, she noticed that the student was not focusing on the lesson topic, but talking about universities. She listened and asked questions to connect his concern about universities to the topic at hand so she could bring the group back around to where she felt it needed to be. Karen notes, "I think a teacher needs to be able to let students voice their personal concerns and interests, but at the same time you've got to connect [discussion] back to the topic you're teaching."

Karen explains that her relationships with students are important to both their learning and growth as individuals. She says, "I am not one of those standoffish teachers" and notes that her students sometimes call her "Mama Shep." They often stop by and see her in the office and sometimes call her at home. She says that what has surprised her in her new position is that seniors need attention as much as, or more than, the younger students because they are "making monumental decisions."

A CLOSE LOOK AT INSTRUCTION

Karen's concern about meeting students where they are naturally connects to her decisions about instruction. She designs lessons and units in which student inquiry and participation is central, because she believes increased learning as well as interest in science will result. Karen believes science is learned best when students become engaged in a messy way—with hands-on experiments and observations that are linked to multiple opportunities for reading, writing, and discussion. Her view of an ideal science curriculum is one in which students are involved in continual inquiry on topics of personal interest. While in the real life of school Karen cannot always make her ideal happen, she does her best to insure that students can really connect to what they are studying.

Planning and Instructional Decision-Making

Karen plans her classes carefully to provide a range of learning experiences for each topic both within a unit of several weeks and within one class period. In a unit on angiosperms, for example, students made extensive observations, completed several labs, wrote lab reports, read a textbook chapter as well as related articles on the topic, participated in cooperative group activities, and used the Internet to locate additional sources and photographs.

During a typical one- or two-hour daily block, Karen provides a variety of experiences to keep students engaged and maximize learning. For example, she generally uses a 15-minute whole-class mini-lesson to introduce a new topic. During this introduction, Karen helps students link the new topic to material they had studied earlier as well as their preparatory reading from the textbook, articles, or a website. Later in the same or a following class, students generally conduct observations and experiments and take notes related to their observations. These notes can include diagrams and pictures in addition to words. The lab is usually followed by writing a formal lab report and participating in discussions related to findings.

On some occasions, Karen says the process might be reversed with the observations/experimentation occurring before the reading or the whole-class session. Overall, Karen feels it is important to use teaching strategies in a flexible way to encourage students' thinking, exploration, and ability to develop concepts and link ideas.

Focus on Literacy

When asked about her students' literacy, Karen notes that as a science educator she thinks of literacy in two ways. First, she believes it is vital for students to become scientifically literate—to understand science concepts and know how to find answers to scientific questions. Second, she also thinks that reading, writing, and discussion are important for learning in the classroom and in the lives of scientists. She hopes her students will develop both science literacy and communication literacy in order to become more knowledgeable and competent as young scientists.

Karen notes that she thinks about her students' reading a great deal, because even her most advanced students need help in coping with both the quantity and difficulty of the reading that is expected of them. Karen is required to use the district-approved textbook, and the state and AP exams require strong knowledge of complex concepts and terminology that are included in the text. In addition to the textbook, Karen teaches students how to explore web-based information and other resources such as journal articles related to topics of study. Additionally, she often makes handouts of information she finds in newspapers or magazines.

Karen notes that for all classes she assigns reading almost every night so that students can gain background knowledge on the topic they are studying. However, Karen also says that it is very important for science teachers to think carefully about exactly how they use texts. She believes text-based learning can become a crutch, on which both teachers and students rely too much for memorization of facts rather than on their own observations. Karen wants her students to think critically about science questions and learn to read to get the information they need for background for a scientific experiment or to answer a scientific question.

Karen says that she is very serious about students reading all of the material she assigns and remarks, "How can I assign a book I haven't read?" She consistently reads everything so she is able to tell students, "I have read everything I have asked you to read, so I know how difficult it is." Noting the heavy conceptual load in the reading for high school students, she clarifies:

> Obviously we have a lot of reading to do in AP. There's so much information in the book and so many new words. For a lot of [students] it is like another language. They have to go back and learn all that. That's a difficulty.

She explains that even students in the advanced AP classes need her support in learning to deal with difficult reading material.

To help students with their reading, Karen says that she has students bring their texts to class and spends time going over sections that present the most difficult concepts. For example, the topic of angiosperm reproduction was very difficult for students to understand. Karen pointed out to students which sections of text included key points on this topic, and had students re-read them in class. The students were then asked to summarize and analyze key points during class discussion. (See the Content Area Handbook for the Summarization Strategies).

Karen also mentions that the Internet is a wonderful source for finding very current information on various topics, although students must be taught to evaluate the source of the information. She recalls that when the class began the section on genetics, there was a lot of information in the press about a gorilla that acted like a cross between a human and an ape. Karen encouraged students to use the genetics material being studied to answer questions posed in the press. This really got them interested. Still, she cautions about the use of the Internet and other information sources because students may simply copy information without truly understanding. She says:

> That's a difficult thing to teach kids. It's not getting there when they are copying somebody else's words. We could debate with kids whether they are cheating or not cheating . . . [but what is really important is] the process involved to get to that information. Just because you have words on the page doesn't mean you have the reason for getting the words on the page.

Overall, Karen feels that the learning and thinking processes gained in her classroom are what is really important and what she wants students to take with them.

Focus on Written Communication

Karen also wants students to learn to use writing to effectively communicate their observations and science learning. She believes that being able to communicate scientific ideas both orally and in writing is very important. She also notes that writing helps students synthesize their learning:

> Students have to [write] four major essays on the AP exams . . . so we do a lot of essays. They write a three or four-page essay for one question. I try to bring in creative writing sometimes to get them to look at [a topic] from an aspect of whatever it is they have done. For example, when they wrote about the process of photosynthesis, they had to pick a molecule that's involved in photosynthesis and write its life cycle. They had to go through how it felt to be part of this molecule—how it felt when it was removed from that molecule—and how it felt to be put here—and how tragic it was. The students say that assignment really helped them to put [the whole process] into their minds.

For most labs, Karen has students do comprehensive written reports. This includes analyzing, graphing and putting the lab into their own words:

> I believe in having my kids write. There's always a conclusion in the lab where they have to relate it back to major concepts. They need to tell me what they did, why they did it and what they did wrong—there's no other way to do that but to write.

Karen says she counts the lab write-ups as a major assignment because the process is so important.

Focus on Discussion

Karen also believes that discussion is a very important tool for learning in her class. However, like many secondary teachers she has found that creating a positive atmosphere for discussion is not easy. One difficulty was that when she tried to hold whole class discussions, smaller discussions often emerged:

> It always seems to break down into itty-bitty discussions everywhere that I couldn't monitor. We'd start off together . . . and I'd just sit by the front table and participate. But the back table would get into one discussion and the front table would get into another discussion [and] there would be little talks going on all the time. It really bothered me when I first started until I realized that they were talking about Biology.

Karen has found that the reason her whole-class discussion sometimes break down into little discussions is that students are asking each other to clarify points before they go on. She says, "A lot of them have really learned how to use another person to help . . . in getting the knowledge. So, [my own] flexibility and not [requiring them to be] all focused in just one discussion at any given time has been a learning experience." In essence, Karen learned from observing her students' discussion behavior that often, small groups focused on specific areas of need or student interest have been more productive than one discussion for the whole class.

Another strategy that Karen has found successful is to divide the class into one discussion group and one lab group. With this plan, she can divide her time more

easily between the groups, which she feels enhances the work of both. Also, going around the room to discuss an activity individually with students is also helpful. For example, when students are doing a drawing to demonstrate a concept, Karen will observe and discuss their individual efforts.

Sensitive Topics

Karen stresses the importance of debate when students have serious questions related to particular topics. For example, when working on the evolution unit, Karen says discussions and debates were common because students had differing views based in part on their religious backgrounds. In the beginning of the unit students were invited to state and discuss their opinions. During the unit ongoing debate was encouraged. However, Karen says

> My job is never to change a child's opinion overall . . . [But] it's hard to stand up there and say, 'I am not talking of your beliefs.' [Actually] that's one of those wonderful discussions we had on 'What's a belief and what's a fact?' Science is based on [evidence] and I want them to develop an appreciation [for science] they might not . . . [otherwise] have.

Karen also notes that open debating is not always possible for two reasons: Students may not have adequate background to discuss the issues or they may not feel safe taking personal risks particularly at the beginning of the semester. To help establish background knowledge and a risk free environment, Karen employs case study debates with role-playing so that students can develop background knowledge and argue a particular point of view without being put on the spot personally.

At the beginning of the botany unit, for example, Karen introduced the issue of whether or not to legislate sustainable agriculture with a case study (see Figure 5-1) and open debate with six roles (see Figure 5-2). To prepare for the debate the students were split into six groups and each group was to prepare a position statement for one

FIGURE 5-1 Case Study Used to Spark Student Discussion About Sustainable Agriculture

CASE STUDY

SUSTAINABLE AGRICULTURE: TO LEGISLATE OR NOT?

The state legislature is considering mandating that alternative agricultural practices be used on all farms in the state by 2010. Alternative farming encompasses, but is not limited to, farming systems referred to as biological, low-input, organic, regenerative, or sustainable. It includes a range of practices such as integrated pest management (IPM); low-intensity animal production systems; crop rotations designed to reduce pest damage, improve crop health, decrease soil erosion, and in the case of legumes, fix nitrogen in the soil; and tillage and planting practices that reduce soil erosion and help control weeds. Sustainable agriculture is an effort to curb erosion by modifying plowing techniques and to protect water supplies by minimizing, If not eliminating, artificial fertilizers and pest controls. The legislature has set up a committee to review the alternative agriculture issue and has charged them with reporting back to the entire legislative body. In order to insure that the committee is able to make the best possible recommendation to the legislative body of the state, they have agreed to hear from several experts in the field of agriculture. The experts presenting information to the committee will be a Soil Conservation Service District Representative, a State Department of Agriculture Representative, a successful farmer using sustainable agricultural methods, a successful farmer using conventional methods, an environmentalist, and an economist. The expert positions are included on a separate page that you may obtain from your teacher.

What options would you recommend that the committee consider investigating? What options would you recommend to the legislative body if you were a member of the committee?

FIGURE 5-2 Description of the Six Roles for Students to Consider in the Sustainable Agriculture Debate

PRESENTERS AND THEIR POSITIONS

The Soil Conservation Service District Representative favors the use of sustainable agricultural usage. The Soil Conservation Service (SCS) currently lends equipment and support to farmers wishing to try the techniques used in low-input sustainable agriculture. It is the theory of the SCS that sustainable agricultural practices replace energy and chemicals with diversity and information. The SCS endorses the use of low-input sustainable agriculture as the best method to control erosion. The SCS District Representative cited a report on the 100 year study of Sanborn Field, on the edge of the campus of the University of Missouri. In this study, where alternative agricultural practices were used, soil erosion was significantly less than in areas where conventional methods were used.

The State Department of Agriculture Representative informed the committee that multiple cropping already accounts for 20% of the world food production. She felt that it was the responsibility of her organization to regulate the agricultural industry and to consider what was the best for all involved. She stated that the primary areas of concern for her department would be that safe, quality products are being placed on the market for the consumer, protecting those who work the land, and in safeguarding the soil and water.

Farmer Abel utilizes no-till farming. He switched from conventional methods four years ago. Currently, he farms 300 acres with the help of two men. Last year his corn yield netted $120.00 per acre. He believes in the potential for this type of agriculture and has had increasingly better yields each of the four years that he has been involved in low-input agriculture. Farmer Abel does not believe that this method is less expensive, but that it creates less contamination.

Farmer Wate uses conventional methods to farm his 1000 acres. He employs the help of three other men. He does not believe that low-input methods allow the farmer to maintain an adequate income and that the sustainable agriculture movement is "returning to the dark ages". Last year his corn yield netted $100.00 per acre (a good year). It is Farmer Wate's belief that he can make up any monetary loss per acre by farming more acreage, and that would not be an alternative if he utilized the low-input methods.

The environmentalist stated that low-input agriculture will help with the erosion problem, ground water contamination problems, and is a more efficient use of energy. He warned that if society does not deal with the problems addressing the world quickly, then we may not have an earth to worry about. He feels that the present global agricultural practices are placing unnecessary pressures on the sustainability of the earth's resources, therefore it is absolutely necessary to mandate a change.

The economist informed the committee that farmers will not save any money using the low-input methods, but that the money is simply spent on different inputs. She indicates that farmers making the switch to low-input agriculture will not witness benefits for three to five years as they are still recouping their initial investments into new equipment needed to employ the sustainable methods. She expressed the need for the state to expand opportunities for new and existing farmers to prosper using sustainable systems should they legislate mandatory methods usage. She stated that reliable information, training and apprenticeship programs, tax incentives, subsidies, grants, and loans would need to be readily available to farmers, extension agents, bankers, and others.

of the roles and questions for the other people on the panel. After 15 minutes of preparation one student from each group came to the front to play a role, and the students remaining in the audience asked the panel questions they had prepared for the debate. Karen acted as the moderator.

A particularly interesting turn of events occurred when students in the audience pretended to be fertilizer and pesticide manufacturers incensed at being left out of the discussion. When the debate was over Karen asked what went well and what could be improved, as they would hold another debate when concluding the botany unit. Karen was delighted when students said they needed more knowledge about plant growth and suggested that a chemical company representative be added to the panel.

Modifications for Special Needs

Karen believes it is important to help students who have particular needs. To Karen, providing the best education possible means sometimes doing things a bit differently for students who have special needs. She discusses Laura, a girl who was very sociable and very involved in learning but who was very slow at taking notes. Karen decided to give Laura a copy of the teacher notes whenever note-taking was done in class. She still required the girl to be involved in writing and listening in the discussion. Karen noted that after giving her the notes, Laura's grade increased because she became less concerned with getting everything written down and more concerned with focusing on what was being learned.

Karen explains, however, that other students may see this type of modification as giving a student an unfair advantage. So she tries to address these issues by helping others realize that some students' needs are different. For example, Karen recalls that a group of students who had not been doing their own notetaking came to her at the end of the unit and wanted a copy of the notes. She refused and told them:

> You haven't done anything in this last two-week period but sit there. You haven't taken your own notes; you haven't added any notes; you haven't come after school on a daily basis to get the notes. You have done nothing and now you want me to hand it to you?

She said the students then began to understand, saying, "We never thought about that!"

WORKING AND GROWING AS A PROFESSIONAL

When asked about how she continues her own professional development, Karen mentions influences both within and outside of her school. She explains that her transition to a student-centered teacher from a content-centered teacher hasn't occurred overnight and notes that for the first six years of her teaching career she focused on presenting content instead of focusing on the students.

> In my first teaching job I worked with someone who thought content was most important and I followed that lead. However, as I took graduate courses that

discussed brain research, learning styles, content reading strategies, and attended faculty development sessions, and saw that my students were only remembering content long enough to take a test, I realized that I had to change my focus.

Karen said her changes in instruction were supported by a principal who pushed for student-centered instruction within the school. She looked up to him as a model and says, "He became a great mentor and a great friend." Karen recalls a year under his mentorship when she was teaching three different biology classes to students who spoke 8 languages and who had a variety of different learning styles. During that year she moved from being more teacher-centered to more student-centered and recalls this as a fabulous learning experience.

Karen also notes the importance of her exposure to information on learning theory and research. When findings from brain research were beginning to come out, she was interested and began to come into her classroom looking more closely at how students learned. She also felt she became a much better teacher when the students knew she cared about them. Karen says, "There are times when knowing the kids and focusing on their learning styles are the only ways I can figure out how to get the information across and help them learn how to process it themselves."

Karen talks about the importance of continued experience and ongoing training and is pleased that her district offers a wide variety of workshops. She says, "To me to be a teacher is to constantly accept learning. I want to learn to be the best teacher I can be for my students so I just eat it all up." Karen explains that the combination of the learning opportunities that the district provides and a good support network of other teachers have had ongoing positive influences on her teaching ability.

Another influence on Karen was a teacher in her graduate program who not only talked about how to teach but also modeled strategies for them. She said that a content reading course was influential because it helped her realize some of the reading comprehension problems some students face and gave her strategies that could be used to help these students.

At the beginning of the current year, Karen consulted with another teacher of AP Biology to schedule topics. The other teacher helped her decide on a sequence of topics and she observed that she does not cover the book in order, but by concept:

> The AP exam which students take at the end of the course is based on certain content and themes. Evolution for example, is one major theme. Passing genetic information is a major theme; and the way molecules behave is another major theme. These themes are tied into most all work done in class.

Although Karen felt fortunate to have the guidance of a colleague who has a successful program, she notes that even with help, deciding what to focus on and how much time to spend on given themes has been a struggle for her. She says:

> Because [students] are assessed by this major tool at the end of the year—the AP exam—it's been really difficult for me. I think I'm going through a learning curve of what's important and what's not important.

Karen has also sought the help of other professionals. For example, she started communicating with college professors who taught Biology. She notes that what is considered important to cover is "constantly shifting. Based on what the state tells us is important, based on what AP tells us is important, and based on what the college and the universities are doing."

Overall, Karen feels that because the ultimate goal is to prepare students for their future, it is important that they have some good basic knowledge of science. She cites mentors, colleagues, graduate courses, workshops, current research, challenging teaching situations, and national/state exams all as having an impact on her decision making in the classroom and growth as a professional.

CONCERNS

Although Karen is experienced and very positive about teaching, she still faces dilemmas related to motivation, time management, and decision-making.

Motivation

One problem Karen sees is lack of motivation for students who are just fulfilling a third year science requirement.

> Some of the kids in [Biology II] can't fit the 2-hour [AP] block into their schedule. But most of the kids aren't really interested in science [and] just take Biology II because they have the third year requirement of science for college entry. So . . . it's been a hard class to get motivated.

Although Karen believes that highly motivational instruction is possible, she shares the following concerns:

> I think one of the problems with really motivational instruction is that you have to know your content to know what's expected, but it's hard to go that way when it is the first year you are teaching something. That's kind of what I've struggled with this year. I don't feel great [confidence] about the exact content I am teaching so it's hard to let the students determine the direction because you really don't know where they are going to take you.

Staying "on Schedule"

Karen says that one of the greatest dilemmas she faces is balancing the amount of time available with the content required and student learning needs. While she obviously wants her students to gain an in-depth understanding of the content, she also is continually faced with the reality that they must take either AP or state exams at the end of the semester, so certain "coverage" is necessary.

Karen plans time carefully, and has developed a good sense of "knowing exactly how long" a particular concept will take. She also credits a colleague in her school with helping her develop this sense of timing. Karen comments:

> I always find it amazing that some teachers are through and there's time left over. That's never ever my problem. My problem is actually cutting some of the activities I planned. I have teachers say, "How do you fill the time?" I think, 'How do you not fill the time?' I think they must present the information one way and one way only. After 14 years I have learned I can't do that. I've got to present it to them, then I've

got to present it to them another way. Then they have to deal with it, and then I come back and present it another way. I used to think I was spoon feeding them, but I learned that I have to help them see different ways to process information. Even as the teacher I have to process information in different ways to really understand it, so helping them understand a variety of ways to process information and how to do it takes more than one day.

Time Management and Student Responsibility

Karen puts some of the burden for time management on her students. She explains that if students fall behind because they have missed a class or not understood something, they know they need to catch up so they can be involved in the next day's discussion or activity. She says that she makes sure students know what they are responsible for and how the class works and notes the importance of bringing closure to the end of every class to reduce confusion. Each day, she tries to give them something to do to direct their learning for the next day.

Karen explains that there is a lot of reading for Biology II homework. She thinks what is difficult for the students in this course to realize is that they are geared towards college and that homework in college is basically reading, keeping up with lectures, and figuring out how to make the knowledge your own. To get them into the habit Karen says:

> I have a lot of procrastinators [who] have been very successful up to this point, but wait until the night before the test to study. This is the first class for many of them where two to five hours the night before the test is not enough. [So] every now and then I give 'em a quiz . . . just to check whether they are trying to keep up with the material.

Karen says that during the first semester of Biology II she worked on helping students schedule their time. She gave due dates for projects and consistently reminded students that although there was not a specific project on the calendar, it didn't mean there was nothing to be done. She encouraged students to keep up with reading and reviewing material on their own. Karen commented that when work was turned in and graded, she even put smiley faces on papers, noting that, "Even seniors love those little stickers."

Dilemmas in Selecting Teaching Strategies

Karen notes that she is trying to avoid using lecture too much because the whole-class format can limit student participation, and she wants students to learn more on their own without being "given everything." She worries that during her first year teaching AP, she has used lecture too much because she has still been developing a sense of how to cover the large amount of required college-level content within the year. Karen believes it is essential that her students develop skills as independent learners, and reminds them that in college, "You are not going to have professors outline everything for you." Thus, even for the experienced professional, balancing support with responsibility and content with process present ongoing challenges.

▰▰ **SUMMING UP** ▰▰▰▰▰▰▰▰▰▰▰▰▰▰▰▰

For Karen, the importance of student-centered learning is paramount. She believes in presenting material in a variety of ways and using appropriate strategies to aid student learning. She is continually trying to find ways to improve her teaching, and believes strongly that students "need to trust me and I need to trust them."

- After reading this chapter, consider the following questions.
  1. What did you find most interesting or surprising when reading this case?
  2. Look back at your answers to the Thought Questions at the beginning of the chapter. How do you think Karen describes teaching biology? How is her description similar to or different from yours?
  3. In your own teaching situation, or one with which you are familiar, would it be possible to teach this way? Why or why not?
  4. Karen included a variety of reading, writing, and oral communication strategies in her instruction. If she wanted to increase her use of literacy even further, what else would you recommend to her?
  5. If you used the *Categorization Strategy*, share your categories with someone in your class or study group. What are the similarities and differences?

- You may wish to use a content area literacy strategy to reflect on this case study. We suggest using the *Summarization Strategy* (see the description in the Handbook, p. 153).

chapter **6**

High School Mathematics

GUIDELINES

Thought Questions Consider the following questions and note your answers in a log or journal.

1. What connections do you make when you hear the phrase "teaching math"?
2. What do you see as the major joys and pains of teaching math?

- Before reading, you may want to engage in a content area literacy strategy. We suggest the *Post-Graphic Organizer* (see description in the Content Area Handbook, p. 142). This strategy helps readers activate background knowledge and provides the teacher with information about students' concepts.
- While reading this chapter, you may wish to continue to use the *Summarization Strategy*. This strategy helps readers reduce a text to its main points (see the description in the Handbook, p. 153).
- National Standards in Math can be found at: http://nctm.org/standards/standards.htm

I t is 7:22 A.M., before school on a Wednesday morning. Sri's high school Algebra I block class is already buzzing with students speaking several languages. Joseph shows his teacher a mathematics word puzzle he downloaded from the World Wide Web the night before. Sri decides to use the puzzle in place of the morning warm-up exercise she had previously planned. She immediately writes the puzzle questions on the board. As the bell rings, Sri directs everyone's attention to the warm-up, which begins the 90-minute double-period class.

Sri is a second-year teacher at this comprehensive, 1300-student Virginia high school located just across the Potomac River from Washington, D. C. "Algebra I Block,"

which meets for two consecutive periods per day, is part of a district-wide initiative to enable all students to succeed in algebra. Students receive two mathematics credits for the course, one in general math, and the other in algebra.

The 21 students in this class have diverse needs. Eleven are members of immigrant families from Latin America, Africa, China, and Morocco, and speak English as their second language. Other students are identified as learning disabled or participate in "Eight-Plus," a district-wide program for students who failed a portion of their eighth grade courses the year before. A learning disabilities teacher teams with Sri and works with the class for 45 minutes each day.

The school is a brick, multilevel building closely surrounded by a well-kept urban/suburban neighborhood of federal government workers, military officers, and other professionals. The student population is both economically and ethnically diverse, including students who live in the neighborhood next to the school and those who live in communities of smaller homes and apartments a few miles away.

As Sri takes attendance, she notices that only 15 of her 21 students are present. Later she learns that two of the absentees had been suspended earlier that morning for stealing calculators. She mentions to an observer that while this is certainly serious, the students had been doing well in class and she hopes they will not be out very long. As Sri circulates around the room to check assignments, she exclaims quietly, "Julie, you've done your homework, I'm so proud!" Julie is a student who had completed little work for several weeks. Sri had met with Julie for over an hour the previous afternoon.

Sri then asks Alan, a student diagnosed with severe ADHD, to pull down the overhead screen in preparation for a whole-group lesson using graphing calculators. Sri attaches her calculator to the projector and asks students to get their individual calculators out of their backpacks. These expensive calculators were purchased earlier in the year through a statewide funding initiative and are signed out to all algebra students. Halfway into the 90 minute class, the learning disabilities teacher joins the class to assist Alan and several other students.

Later in the day, Sri teaches 3 more classes, including a more traditional Algebra I class and two functions classes for college-bound juniors and seniors. All of these classes meet 5 class periods per week, while the Algebra I block class meets 10 periods per week. Sri teaches in two different classrooms on the second floor of her school. Each room is shared with other teachers and is equipped with traditional one-piece desks and blackboards. In both rooms, Sri and other math teachers display examples of student work on bulletin boards and on ropes hanging from the ceiling. Most of these projects include artwork and show connections between mathematics and other subject areas.

MEETING SRI

Sri was only in her second year of teaching when we first met her. We visited several times that year, and again at the end of her third year to learn about her perspective over time.

When asked about her background, Sri explained that she grew up in Kansas and Pennsylvania in a family of Indian descent. Interestingly, Sri says that in high school she hated math and "never understood it." She remembers that high school mathematics was taught by lecture with little student participation. Later, while an undergraduate at the American University, Sri took more mathematics as part of her major in theoretical economics. At this point she began to enjoy the subject. Although not enrolled in teacher education, as a college senior Sri started to think about becoming a teacher when she worked as a teaching assistant for a freshman economics course.

After college, Sri worked for The Associated Press in the area of television and radio marketing. After several years, she decided to return to school full time to complete a master's degree and obtain teaching licensure. Sri says her father recommended that she teach mathematics, and she reasoned that she might become a good math teacher in part because of her own difficulty with the subject in high school. Her master's program included a one-year full time internship in a diverse high school just outside Washington, D.C. After completing this program, Sri began her current position in a nearby school.

INSIDE SRI'S CLASSROOM

Sri's classroom is a busy place. Sri changes activities frequently, both to keep student attention and to provide diverse experiences that increase learning. She says she never lectures for more than 15 minutes, and expects students to contribute, ask questions, and take notes when she does. She finds that note-taking not only provides students a record of the lecture but also serves to keep their attention and increases learning. Sri's philosophy is that the more students use various forms of communication—writing, purposeful discussion, and reading/interpretation of both graphics and print—the more they will learn.

While Sri was not familiar with the term "content literacy" when we first began our interviews, she was knowledgeable about NCTM (National Council of Teachers of Mathematics) Standards (2000) related to mathematics communication and classroom discourse. Throughout each class period she expects students to use language in a variety of ways to learn mathematics. Students must interpret and communicate mathematical ideas in written, oral, pictorial, and graphic forms. As Sri says,

> I don't teach math using math language. It's very different. [I] teach it in English and then go to the mathematics language [symbols and terms]. I always say 'math is a foreign language.'

Sri also believes strongly in the importance of students' conceptual understanding in mathematics. She wants students to link their mathematics learning to knowledge in other content areas, such as geography. In addition, Sri believes all students need to see real life applications of mathematics, and that they need to see how the mathematics they learn in one course connects to the mathematics they learned previously or will learn in the future. Sri also believes that students need support in finding the sequence and connections among mathematical ideas and between mathematics and other subjects:

I try to show all of the connections and teach math very sequentially. [For example], when I taught arithmetic sequences [to the functions classes], I brought out the Algebra I book and I said, 'Look, this is [the same thing as] slope. This is the same thing as a y intercept. This is y equals $mx + b$. You guys know this in your sleep.' [I want them to] bring the connections in. It's not all that foreign, new or different. [The new material] is often just a variation on the same thing.

A CLOSE LOOK AT INSTRUCTION

Like most teachers, Sri makes instructional decisions both well in advance and also on the fly as each class evolves. She works to scaffold or support students' learning by carefully structuring concept presentations from easier to more difficult. She also tries to ensure that students understand one concept before they move to the next. This ongoing assessment sometimes requires that Sri change and adjust what is taught to meet students' needs on a given day.

As an example, in the Algebra block class described earlier, the lesson sequence included a warm-up exercise in which students found solutions to problems related to drawing lines on graphs, which had been introduced the day before. Students were permitted to use either graph paper or their graphing calculators for this exercise. Sri then moved to a whole-class introduction for the next part of the concept. For demonstration, she attached her graphing calculator to the overhead projector to show an enlarged version of what students were seeing on their small calculators (Figure 6-1). Instruction on *how* to use the calculators was an integral part of the lesson.

As follow-up, students were asked to work in pairs and use their calculators to solve additional problems. Sri gave each pair a large sheet of chart paper so they

FIGURE 6-1   Sri Leads the Think-Pair-Share Activity

could record their answers and share them with the entire class at the end of the period. This teaching strategy is sometimes called a "Think-Pair-Share," because students think on their own, collaborate with a partner, and then share with a larger group (see the Handbook, p. 154).

Connections and Concepts

Sri also works to help students connect learning from one day to the next through both explicit and subtle strategies. At several points in each lesson she helps students make these links. For example, she might tell students: "So far this year we have talked about . . . ," and gives a description of concepts already learned that connect to the current concept. She also gives alternatives so that students begin to understand mathematical complexity, for example: "There is another way we can write the equation for a line . . . ," and gives an example.

Frequently, Sri will explain to students that mathematics is more conceptual than numeric —"You don't even have to do arithmetic anymore . . . we are *beyond* arithmetic." She also emphasizes concepts rather than memorization when teaching mathematics vocabulary by embedding the instruction into her lesson rather than addressing vocabulary as something separate. For example, when showing the calculator-generated graph in Figure 6-1, Sri *asks* students, "What is this called?" rather than *telling* them it is a parabola. While these subtleties in questioning techniques may seem minor, over time an inquiry-oriented environment develops in which students realize they are expected to think for themselves.

Another subtle technique Sri uses is to move around the room when students are working independently. In this way she can make informal assessments of progress and gear her presentation accordingly. For example, when Algebra I students use graphing calculators, Sri cannot see the results of their work because the calculators do not have a printing capacity. Briefly checking each student's calculator screen gives Sri informal assessment data during a lesson. She also sometimes asks students to transfer their results to graph paper.

Sri finds that movement around the classroom also helps students realize that she is interested in their progress, which encourages on-task behavior. She uses explicit verbal reminders to let students know they are expected to stay engaged throughout the class period, such as, "I want to see everyone making an X and Y, and plotting those 3 points." These techniques are particularly important in the algebra block class, where many students have extremely short attention spans or other special needs.

Expanding Understanding

With her advanced-level functions classes, Sri places an even greater emphasis on higher-order thinking and independence. For these juniors and seniors, college is not far off. Sri explains that she tries "to get [students] to understand the big concepts before we get into the nitty-gritty [of problem solving]." However, she finds students are often resistant to independence because it is new to them: "They want me to give them the formula. They want me to show them how to do [every] problem, and I don't want to do that."

Sri sometimes jokes with students about their resistance, at the same time insisting that they put forth their best efforts:

> [When they ask how to do a problem], I say, 'What do you think?' They say, 'Why can't you just show us how to do it?' I say, 'I don't want to show you how to do it. That would just take all of the fun away from my life.'

Sri wants her students to become independent thinkers and says she tells them that she can't "teach [them] how to do every single problem in the world." Instead, she hopes to teach some methodology so that they can later be successful at calculus, which has "few hard and fast rules."

To assist her advanced students in this learning process, Sri encourages a study strategy in which students take notes in class and then ". . . go home and rewrite them and look at them again and see the gaps and discover [answers]." With this group, Sri sometimes intentionally lectures and skips steps "like a college professor," expecting students to review on their own and figure out the process. Sri says that over time, many students do come to see the value of learning more independently, although they find it difficult. She mentions one student who resisted at the beginning, but told Sri excitedly in April that "this [study system] really works [because] now I understand [the mathematics] better than ever!"

SPECIAL PROJECTS AND ASSIGNMENTS

Over the course of the year, Sri does a number of special projects and assignments with both groups of students. Typically, these activities involve work over several days or weeks, with the purpose of linking several mathematical concepts with those in other areas of study. Examples include the slope project completed by Algebra I students, the time zone project completed by the functions students, and two group projects.

Algebra I: The Slope Project

Sri says that her slope project is a common project used by many mathematics teachers. Students are given ten different slope values, which indicate a change in the *y* axis divided by a change in the *x* axis. They must plot these lines on a graph and create a coherent picture using all of them. Sri explains that "the lines can be any length, but they have to have that particular slope."

Sri introduces this project in a gradual and inductive way. First, she introduces the concept of *slope* by connecting this term to students' understanding of *rates of change* in everyday life. Students work with partners to solve common problems ("At 3:00 P.M., a car leaves a city. By 5:00 P.M., it has traveled 90 miles. Find its average speed."). After students have solved several similar problems, she asks them to write a formula "that could be used to find any rate."

Over several weeks, Sri helps students learn to graph rate changes on paper and on their graphing calculators (see Figure 6-2). They advance to plotting slope lines on graph paper through several whole-class and small group "fun" exercises in which pictures are created when lines are correctly drawn (see Figure 6-3). For these lessons, Sri models with several examples, using the overhead projector. She then assigns students to work in small groups and to assist one another in completing additional examples. They also practice plotting lines on their graphing calculators.

Students then are assigned an individual project to complete at home, in about two weeks. This project requires that they take one assigned slope value and create a variety of lines that form a coherent picture.

Sri believes this assignment requires a more advanced understanding of *slope* because students must both visualize the lines and create a cohesive order. Above

FIGURE 6-2   Instructions for the Slope Project

SLOPE PICTURES   USE A STRAIGHT EDGE TO DRAW ALL LINES!
ALGEBRA 1

#1: USE GRAPH WITH WAVES AT THE BOTTOM

1) From the point (0, 13), draw a line with a slope of $-4/3$, 4 slopes long.

2) From the ending point of the above line segment, draw a line with a slope of $-1/-6$, 2 slopes long.

3) From the ending point of the previous line segment, draw a line with a slope of $2/-5$. 1 slope long.

4) From the ending point of the previous line segment, draw a line with a slope of 3. Make it 5 slopes long.

5) You should be at the point (0,12). Check to see that you have drawn the above lines correctly.

6) From the point (0, -8), draw a line with a slope that is undefined. Make it 21 units long.

7) From the point (-13, -8), draw a line with a slope of 0. Make it 26 units long.

8) From the point (-13, -8), draw a line with a slope of $-5/2$, 1 slope long.

9) From the ending point of the previous line segment, draw a slope of $2/-5$, 2 slopes long.

10) From the ending point of the previous line segment, draw a slope of $1/3$, 4 slopes long.

11) From the ending point of the previous line segment, draw a slope of $5/2$, 1 slope long.

12) You should have ended at the point (13, -8). What is your picture?

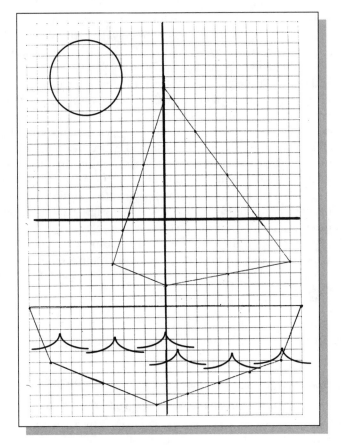

FIGURE 6-3   Student's Picture Resulting From the
Slope Project

all, she wants students to see connections. She explains that she is "... big on connecting the algebra with the graph ... so they can say 'this is what it would look
like.'" Sri indicates that her students find the project motivating because they enjoy
the chance to be creative. They tend to get very involved in the assignment and are
"able to do it really well." An example of a final project appears in Figure 6-4.

Functions: The Time Zone Project

Sri asks her functions students to complete a similar project related to trigonometry
graphs. This project has a multidisciplinary focus, emphasizing geography. Students
are assigned to graph the numbers of hours of daylight for cities in different parts
of the world. Sri finds that many students have never heard of the cities assigned to
them, and is concerned that even her advanced juniors and seniors seem very lack-
ing in geography knowledge: "I don't think a single kid knew where Jakarta was.
Even when I told them it was in Indonesia [they asked], 'Where's that?'"

FIGURE 6-4 Student's Final Product From the Slope Project

For this project, students must compute the number of hours of daylight for their city, on the winter and summer solstice on the equinox. The result is a sinusoidal function, a function produced by stretching or shifting the sine function.

Sri talks with students about the importance of this information, which frequently is used by air traffic controllers, customs officials, and others who must estimate whether times of arrival will occur during daylight hours. Students also learn details related to differences in seasons around the globe.

In preparing students before the project, Sri divides students into groups and requires each group to "come up with equations" related to four different cities. Students then complete individual poster assignments (see Figures 6-5), which are hung in the classroom. Although she does not require each student to make a formal presentation, Sri and the author of each poster explain details to the class. The

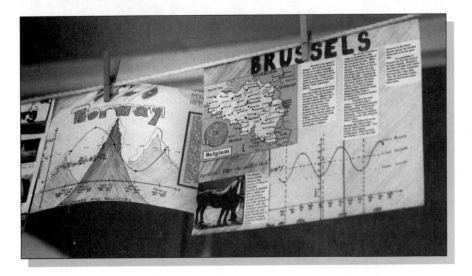

FIGURE 6-5   Students' Time Zone Projects on Jakarta and Brussels

class then makes comparisons across cities. Sri also takes time to discuss geographic and cultural aspects related to the countries students have portrayed.

Project Assessment

Sri uses scoring guides to grade both projects (see the example for the slope project in Figure 6-6). Typically, 50% of 100 points is given for mathematics accuracy (such as 5 points for each correct slope). The other 50% of the points is split in various ways depending on Sri's goals. In Algebra I, Sri generally gives points for following

FIGURE 6-6 Slope Project Assessment Guide

SLOPE PROJECT POINTS   NAME _____

Accuracy   **Following directions**
(50 points or 5 points for each correct slope)   (25 points)

1) m = 0 _____   2) m = undefined _____   Title   _____

3) m = 1/3 _____   4) m = -1/2 _____   Poster Board   _____

5) m = 3 _____   6) m = -7/2 _____   Graph Paper   _____

7) m = 3/4 _____   8) m = 4 _____   Slopes Written _____

9) m = -8/3 _____   10) m = -2/5 _____   Circles/Half   _____

TOTAL   _____   TOTAL   _____

Neatness   _____   **Creativity** _____
(10 points)   (15 points)

TOTAL SCORE

directions, while she does not do so in functions. On the other hand, for functions students, grades are based in part on their geography knowledge, because Sri really "wants them to learn something about the country." Students also receive points for creativity and presentation of their concept.

Students always know at the beginning of a project how it will be graded, as Sri usually spends "a good twenty minutes going over projects when [she] assign[s] them." She shows an outline of each project on the overhead and discusses it with students. She also shows them examples from past years, and notes that she finds it important to give directions that are very clear.

Group Assignments

Sri uses a variety of partner and group in-class assignments that require students to think critically and communicate with one another about mathematics. Sri believes strongly in the value of students working together and explaining concepts to each other, as "you never really know something until you have to teach it to someone else." While some of Sri's group assignments are highly structured long-term assignments, many are planned for a short period of time within one class period.

Figure 6-7 contains instructions for an in-class activity that Sri uses when teaching the algebraic concept called "Exponential Growth and Decay." Students work with partners to complete the experiments described in the instructions. The first, illustrative of an exponential decay model, involves a careful sorting and recording

process using M&Ms. The second experiment illustrates a linear model, while the third experiment illustrates an exponential growth model. The questions at the end of the assignment require students to think critically about their results by applying definitions and making comparisons among models. These questions also require students to explain their answers in written prose. The bonus question pushes learning a step further by asking students to translate their findings to a mathematical equation. Thus, through one apparently simple but carefully constructed assignment, students must communicate with each other to conduct mathematical experiments. They also must convert and explain their findings using graphs, written English, and mathematical symbols. Sometimes they also use graphing calculators while completing this assignment.

Another example of group work in Sri's class is an end-of-year review project in which students write problems for one another to solve. In this two-part assignment, each group first designs a poster that illustrates a mathematics theme or concept. The purpose of the poster is to help students "jog [one another's] memories of different concepts taught in the course." Each group then creates five problems related to the theme, with answers. Of these, Sri picks the best problems and copies them for everyone to use for review.

During her first year of teaching, Sri also had students in both courses write questions for their own final exams. While she felt this worked very well, she explained that it was not possible any longer as the mathematics department had decided to give a departmental exam. Sri has coped with this change by assigning different parts or sections of the book to students and asking them to come up with two questions. As a faculty member she is asked to submit questions for the departmental exam, and selects a few of the best student-created problems. Sri tells students that if she chooses their question, then they will get two extra credit points on the exam. Sri believes that students think more deeply about mathematics when they have to write questions. She says they also learn that a teacher's job is harder than it looks, because "it's not easy to come up with word problems."

EXPONENTIAL GROWTH AND DECAY
ALGEBRA 1

EXPERIMENT: You have a cup full of M&Ms. Count them. Gently lay the M&Ms out on your desk. Take away any M&Ms that do not have the M&M symbol showing. Count the remaining M&Ms and return them to the cup. Lay out the remaining M&Ms and again discard those without the symbol showing. Again count the remaining M&Ms and return them to the cup. Continue this process 10 times. Record your data below.

Trial	M&Ms Remaining
1	
2	
3	
4	
5	
6	
7	
8	
9	
10	

Graph your results: Trials on the x-axis.

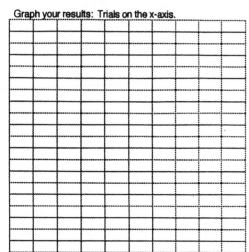

2) You have a secret which is too good to keep to yourself, so you tell one person. The next day he tells one person. The day after she tells another person. Assume nobody tells the secret to someone who already knows. Fill in the chart showing how many people know the secret every day for ten days, and show the results on a graph which compares the day to the total number of people who know.

Day	New People	Total Who Know
1	1	2 (you and who you told)
2	1	3
3		
4		
5		
6		
7		
8		
9		
10		

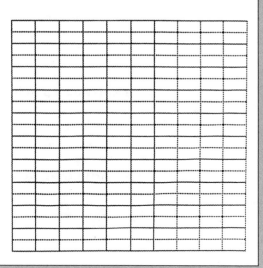

FIGURE 6-7 Exponential Growth and Decay Activity Handout *(continued)*

3) Now you know an even better secret. You tell two friends. Each of them tells two of their friends, who tell two friends, who tell two friends, and so on. Fill in the chart and show the results on a graph which compares the day to the total number of people who know.

Day	New People	Total Who Know
1	2 (the two you told)	3 (you and the two you told)
2	4 (each told two)	7
3	8	
4		
5		
6		
7		
8		
9		
10		

4) The problems above include a linear model, an exponential growth model, and an exponential decay model. Which problem goes with which model? Explain your answer.

5) What are some of the differences between the exponential models and the linear model?

6) What is the major difference between an exponential growth model and an exponential decay model?

BONUS: Write the equation for each of the three problems.

FIGURE 6-7

WORKING AS A PROFESSIONAL

Even though Sri is only in her second year of teaching, she has had many opportunities to interact professionally both in her own school and beyond. Within her school, Sri says that teachers in her department share a lot. For her functions classes, she team-plans with her department chair, who teaches the same course. Sri says that they teach the course "exactly the same; same homework, same everything."

One difficulty with team planning is a lack of time to meet. Sri notes that while sometimes she and her team partner meet after school, weeks go by in which they don't meet but just talk briefly and "trade off," or take turns with planning different lessons. Sri also mentions that within the department as a whole, teachers may have different philosophies but try to use this to the students' advantage. For example, Sri says she is a very calculation-based teacher, and that this fits well with the new state standards in mathematics. Another teacher who has not generally taught in this way has asked Sri for assistance. In summing up relationships in the department, Sri says "we play off each other." She goes on to explain that while during the previous year there seemed to be less sharing, at this point the philosophy of the department was that everyone should not "reinvent the wheel." Sri believes that sharing teaching ideas gives everyone different perspectives and ultimately benefits the students.

Sri frequently talks with other teachers in her department to gain ideas for teaching in creative ways. In addition, she consults books and other materials published by NCTM, her district curriculum guides, sources on the World Wide Web, and her own imagination. As illustrated at the beginning of the chapter, Sri also uses materials brought in by students.

Even though only in the very beginning of her career, Sri is already involved in several major professional service activities beyond her school. She has worked on a project of the National Academy for the Advancement of Sciences that involved comparing and making recommendations about different Algebra I and middle school mathematics curriculums. She also serves on a district-wide curriculum committee for the development of advanced algebra courses. While this type of work is time-consuming, Sri believes these projects are valuable and finds her own participation professionally rewarding.

CONCERNS

Although Sri became a teacher through an extensive preparation program and enjoys her work, she still has concerns and faces dilemmas on a daily basis.

One issue that concerns Sri relates to aspects of teaching she believes "no one preps anybody for [such as] the sheer mountains of paperwork and the loose ends you have to tie on a regular basis." Sri makes an interesting analogy, saying that teaching is a lot like waiting on tables, which she did in college:

> Everything happens really fast. Get through it. Make sure you don't mess up. Make sure everybody gets their food. You're done. You're through, and all of a sudden it's over. And they're gone. Teachers are thinking a lot on their feet. Teaching is a lot of flexibility. The amount of flexibility you need is probably the toughest thing. There are always a few things you have to adjust and change.

Sri also expresses concern about her students' lack of knowledge beyond their own cultural experiences. As noted earlier, she has taken steps to remedy this within her own curriculum but still finds some of their comments surprising. For example, during Roshashana, the Jewish New Year, some of her Christian students asked Sri whether it was 1999 or 2000 on the Jewish calendar, not realizing that those dates are based on the birth of Christ. On another occasion, Sri says students asked if she would be going home for Christmas. She told them she would, but that she did not celebrate Christmas because she wasn't Christian. Students seemed very surprised, and showed even more confusion by then asking if she was Protestant. Sri finds it hard to believe that these juniors and seniors "know so little about religions and culture," especially since they live in a very culturally diverse region adjacent to Washington, D. C.

Another issue of concern to Sri and other teachers throughout Virginia are new state-mandated tests in high school subjects that students must pass for graduation. During the first year of test implementation (her second year of teaching), Sri had to modify instruction to make sure she covered topics on the test by the time it was administered in April. The use of graphing calculators in Algebra I was also required by the new Standards of Learning and related tests. While Sri supports high standards, like many teachers she was concerned about the nature of the tests, their implementation schedule, and whether the test items reflect the NCTM Standards (2000) that had guided curriculum development.

To cope with preparing students for the assessment while avoiding becoming unduly stressed about it, Sri has implemented a method of teaching strategies for test-taking during the last 10 minutes of class for a 3-week period before the state assessment. She finds that her students especially needed practice and guidance in answering multiple-choice questions, as this is not a format she generally uses in her classroom. After Sri implemented this practice her students became more successful test-takers and did very well on the state assessment. Sri believes that their knowledge, gained throughout the year, was very sound, but that learning test-taking strategies was also important to their success on this particular assessment. She remains concerned, however, that the multiple choice format of the state assessment seems in conflict with mathematics educators' views of best assessment practices in mathematics, as delineated in the NCTM Standards and other publications.

SUMMING UP

In her first few years of teaching, Sri has already faced many challenges successfully. She clearly enjoys working with her students, regardless of their personal backgrounds or previous knowledge of mathematics. The overall impression she gives observers and her supervisors is one of high creativity, concern, and commitment. She is devoted to helping students learn both mathematics and more about the world around them. In the process, students use language and literacy in a wide variety of ways.

- After reading this chapter, consider the following questions. You may wish to write your ideas in your journal or discuss them with others.

  1. What did you find most interesting or surprising when reading this case?

  2. Look back at your answers to the Thought Questions at the beginning of the chapter. How do you think Sri describes teaching math? How is her description similar to or different from yours?

  3. In your own teaching situation, or one with which you are familiar, would it be possible to teach this way? Why or why not?

  4. Sri included a variety of reading, writing, and oral communication strategies in her instruction. If she wanted to increase her use of literacy even further, what else would you recommend to her?

  5. If you used the *Summarization Strategy*, share your summary with someone in your class or study group. What are the similarities and differences between your and others' summaries?

- You may wish to use a content area literacy strategy to reflect on this case study. We suggest creating a *Progressive Cinquain* (see the description in the Handbook, p. 144).

chapter 7

High School English

GUIDELINES

Thought Questions   Consider the following questions and note your answers in a log or journal.

1. What connections do you make when you hear the phrase "teaching English"?
2. What do you see as the major thrill and nuisance of teaching English?

- Before reading, you may want to engage in a content area literacy strategy. We suggest the *Your Own Questions Strategy* (see the description in the Content Area Handbook, p. 155). This strategy helps readers engage in active comprehension and resolve their own conceptual conflicts.
- While reading this chapter, you may wish to continue to use a *Double Entry Journal* and see if your questions are answered by the text (see the Handbook, p. 135).
- National Standards in English can be found at: www.ncte.org/standards/standards.shtml

Leslie teaches high school English in a rural community near Dallas, Texas, that is gradually becoming more densely populated. Danville High School, with about 300 students in grades 9–12, is a modern building surrounded by open ranch land. Leslie's students come from families with widely varying levels of education and types of employment. They also are culturally and linguistically diverse. About 20% are Hispanic, about 10% are African American, and about 70% are European American.

Leslie's schedule includes six fifty-minute classes per day. During the year we met with her, she taught four sections of 12th grade British literature, one section of 10th grade English, and one 11th/12th grade elective course entitled "Humanities and World Literature." Her class sizes varied dramatically, ranging from 7 to 23 students.

Students in Leslie's classes have a wide range of academic abilities and needs. While students in her two honors classes generally read above grade level and are college bound, many other students struggle with their high school assignments, and some drop out of school before 12th grade. Some students with special education needs are mainstreamed into Leslie's classes, and receive additional support from special education teachers.

MEETING LESLIE

Leslie was a 4th year teacher at Danville and was completing a master's degree in reading at a local university at the time of her interviews. Before arriving in Texas, Leslie taught for three years in Uganda and three years in a private Christian high school in California. While she greatly enjoys her work as a teacher, Leslie admits that in high school she did not enjoy her classes and told others, "I will never be a teacher." Nonetheless, she took several teacher education courses in college along with her degree in history and English. As a young college graduate Leslie first started teaching for practical reasons, because she did not know of "anything else [she] could do" with her degree.

Early on in Leslie's teaching career, however, she started to realize she had made the right choice. She found that teaching gave her an opportunity to focus on subjects she cared about; she also discovered that she enjoyed working with adolescent learners:

> I love my subject matter . . . but teaching is more than just transferring information. There has to be some kind of relationship between the students and myself. High school students are going through so much turmoil . . . their lives are like one big roller coaster. I see myself as being a stable force. They can come into my room and be safe, calm, and learn something that's going to help them in life.

Like most teachers, Leslie has deeply rooted values and beliefs about teaching that spring from her personal experiences. For example, she credits her mother with helping her develop a love of reading and becoming a lifelong reader: "From an early age she took us to the library once a week, made a big outing of it." Leslie also notes ways her own teachers have influenced her current theories and practices. For example, she describes a college history teacher who influenced her beliefs about student involvement in the learning and assessment process:

> He would sit down with the class and we would make up 5 or 6 essay questions. Then we would decide which 2 essay questions would be on the final exam. We could write about either one and we could bring in a page of notes if we needed them. [But], we could not just recite facts; we had to show that we could take an idea and draw a conclusion.

Overall, Leslie thinks her background experiences both in and out of school provided her with a variety of understandings that undergird her teaching decisions.

INSIDE LESLIE'S CLASSROOM

Leslie sees English/language arts instruction as naturally interdisciplinary. In order to create a curriculum that helps students use language effectively, she blends reading, writing, speaking, listening, and other forms of communication in classwork and assignments. In addition, Leslie stresses the importance of studying language and literature within the framework of other disciplines, such as history and geography.

Leslie says that one of her primary goals is to help students grow in their knowledge of themselves and others, both within and beyond their small town. She worries that many Danville students have never been able to "go places and see things" like more affluent young people. Leslie works to expand their knowledge through a combination of assignments, class activities, and outside experiences. For example, for several years she has taken her humanities class to nearby Dallas for an opera, which she says is often "completely out of their experience." Leslie finds that by preparing the class in advance, students are able to understand the opera, and also notes that she finds it "lovely to see [students] experience" this art form.

Overall, Leslie strongly believes that students' background knowledge develops through a variety of experiences both within and outside the classroom. In addition to the study of opera and other forms of drama and music, she includes lessons on history and world cultures in her teaching of literature. Students also study how language evolves over time, and connect this to their study of the vocabulary and language forms used in different literary works.

In order to develop her curriculum and make it come together each year, Leslie uses a detailed system of planning. Over the course of a year, she develops course, unit, and individual class plans that include carefully selected teaching strategies designed to increase comprehension and learning.

A key aspect of Leslie's thinking is that it is more important to help students gain a depth of understanding about a manageable number of concepts and time periods than to achieve only a surface grasp of a large number of topics. Her district's policies and curriculum allow her some flexibility when making instructional decisions, so she can gear her decisions to the needs of her students. For example, although British literature classes at her school have an assigned text, Leslie is able to be selective about which portions to use. She notes:

> I skip [some of the] time periods covered in the anthology because it has 12 units and I obviously can't cover it all. Just deciding that I'm not going to cover the whole book takes most of the stress out of it. I've never had an administrator say, 'You have to cover this book.'

In deciding which literature selections to use, Leslie picks out pieces she thinks students need to know and would be interested in and also considers which she herself likes best. In addition to the course text and other materials Leslie assigns, students often use supplemental materials they self-select.

In our discussions with Leslie, we focused on her 12th grade British literature classes, which made up most of her schedule. When planning this course, Leslie organizes her year into units related to historical time periods in Great Britain. During the year she teaches 6 six-week units. Topics for five units relate to historical time periods, such as Anglo-Saxon or medieval literature. A sixth unit is focused on completing a research paper.

When planning each 6-week unit, Leslie says she sits down with all of her materials and a big calendar. She decides exactly what she wants students to know and do by the end of the unit. She bases these decisions on her own knowledge of her students and the subject matter, and her district and state curriculum guidelines. She explains that at first she plans "in big chunks, not in detail," but that as the unit progresses she makes plans more detailed. In addition, she sometimes "adds things at the spur of the moment." Leslie believes that planning is never finished, because teachers need to observe and assess students' learning on a continuous basis, and change plans as necessary.

A CLOSE LOOK AT INSTRUCTION

Leslie uses a variety of teaching strategies to achieve her goals. At the beginning of each unit, she pays particular attention to her students' motivation and background knowledge on the new topic. Initial lessons are designed to help students connect the new material to something already familiar. For example, when the class was preparing to read *The Return of the Native* (Hardy, 1940), Leslie began by asking students about their favorite soap opera plots:

> We talked about the twists and turns of soap opera plots. I told them that *Return of the Native* is very much like a soap opera. [In general] I try to pull out things that I think will catch their interest and emphasize those before instruction [because then] they'll be looking for that as they read.

Leslie also has a pattern or framework for beginning class sessions each day. Most classes start with a "sponge," or short activity to focus student attention. A sponge may be a grammar mini-lesson in which students work in groups proofreading writing that is keyed to a particular grammar rule, or a writer's notebook activity in which students write for 5 minutes on a question related to the day's discussion topic. Students later are asked to share ideas from their writing during class discussion.

After the sponge activity, on many days students spend time reading, taking notes, and discussing what was read. Leslie also frequently includes art, oral interpretation, and drama in her instruction. She finds these venues help expand her students' understanding of literature and also provide multiple avenues for success for students with diverse interests and backgrounds.

One day in January, for example, Leslie's class was studying *Hamlet*. Students first participated in small group discussions in which they were asked to identify symbolism in the play. Each group then selected a symbol to illustrate on a poster (see Figure 7-1). After creating the poster, each group acted out their symbol for the class, with the expectation that the class would guess the symbol from the dramatic presentation. Leslie later brought the groups together to discuss all of the symbols that had been located and dramatized. This provided a summary and closure to the lesson, which Leslie thinks is essential for learning and retention.

FIGURE 7-1   Students' Poster Illustrations of Literary Symbols in *Hamlet*

Scaffolding New Experiences

Leslie's major goal for all students is to increase reading comprehension and interest in reading. She finds this a particular challenge with the content of the British literature course, since much of the material is difficult even for advanced students. To bridge the gap between students' reading comfort zones and difficult texts, Leslie carefully structures their interactions with new material in order to support, or "scaffold," their learning. One thing she does is help students connect new ideas with things they knew before. As Leslie notes,

> It's often difficult with the literature to make those connections, but you can always find something they can connect to. With Beowulf, there's a monster, so we talk about different kinds of monsters. If we're doing Shakespeare, they already [have read] *Romeo and Juliet*, which is a tragedy, so I try to connect this to *Macbeth*.

Leslie goes on to discuss how she also helps students use what they already know to learn new vocabulary:

> One set of vocabulary [in the textbook] has personality types such as "melancholic" and "phlegmatic." I tell my students to write down the name of a person they know who is melancholy or phlegmatic, to make a connection with what they already know—their prior knowledge.

Leslie teaches vocabulary both from students' reading materials and from a supplemental book that includes word histories. Students often like to read about word derivations and find that knowing a word's origins often helps them understand and remember difficult vocabulary.

When asked about how she solves other problems she encounters when teaching with difficult texts, Leslie notes that most of her students have trouble understanding the antiquated language in British literature classics. She located useful information in an NCTE (National Council of Teachers of English) publication that helped her to understand what was confusing her students and to develop appropriate interventions:

> For example, in a sentence [Shakespeare] will have a subject and bunch of descriptors, phrase after phrase after phrase of descriptors, and then the verb. For kids to understand they must realize that they have to wait for the verb until he gets through all of his descriptors. When they are able to find the subject and the verb and tear out all the other stuff, they get the gist.

Other examples of teaching strategies Leslie uses to scaffold students' reading comprehension include combining written texts, video, discussion, and notetaking while teaching *Macbeth*:

> I have a video of the play that is almost word for word. We watch the video with our books open. Students take notes and at the end of every scene we stop and discuss what happened. At that point I am concerned that they understand what's happening.

Leslie goes on to explain that after students gain a working understanding of the difficult material, she provides extension activities:

> Later, I might give a writing assignment, like a character study where they come up with three characteristics of *Macbeth* and support the characteristics with examples from throughout the play. I also often have students rewrite a scene in modern language and then present it to the class.

Leslie realizes that students will enjoy and comprehend literature more as they develop fluency. To accomplish this, she sometimes asks students to memorize and perform parts of literature, plays, or poetry. Repeated readings and rehearsal of the text enable even students with reading difficulties to find success in this activity, and Leslie finds that her students enjoy the challenge. She remarks, "I have had [my 12th grade students] memorize the first eighteen lines of the *Prologue to The Canterbury Tales* in Middle English. I like the idea of challenging them with something that they think they cannot do."

Focus on Discussion

Discussions in Leslie's class provide an important opportunity for students to express and clarify their own viewpoints and hear each other's ideas. Leslie believes that discussions facilitate comprehension and learning related to literature. She also thinks that strengthening oral communication is an important language arts goal. Like many teachers, however, Leslie sometimes finds that discussions can be difficult to implement successfully: "I get bothered by the noise and chaos of several people talking at once, which tends to happen. I'm still working on that." Leslie has found it vital to plan class discussions carefully in advance, and to systematically teach students ground rules and give credit for active participation.

Leslie also uses a variety of strategies that link writing, reading, and discussion. For example, during the *Macbeth* unit one discussion related to Lady Macbeth's guilt. At the beginning of the class period, students were asked to reflect on and define "guilt" in their writer's notebooks. Later in the period students shared their writing and discussed their ideas with a small group. The following week, they completed a character study on Lady Macbeth and wrote a formal essay on her guilt feelings. They also used the same personal reflection/sharing/discussion process when considering the concept of violence and the character Macbeth.

Strategic Teaching and Learning

Each year Leslie selects several content reading and learning strategies to use with her students. Her ultimate goal is that students will comprehend the difficult texts used in class and also become more strategic in their reading, writing, and learning.

For example, when teaching students how to approach a research paper, Leslie often uses a "Think Aloud" strategy to model her own process as a reader and writer. During one class, she uses the overhead projector to model ways to summarize text material on notecards. First she draws a blank notecard on a transparency and shows where to put bibliographic information on the card. She then takes a sample reference material, reads a portion of it aloud, and "thinks aloud" or talks through how she makes mental decisions about what to write on each card. Next, she writes this information on the sample card. As a follow-up, when students are creating their own notecards, Leslie circulates around the room and asks individual students to explain their thinking or decision-making about what to write on their own cards. Leslie finds that over time, this process helps students avoid the common traps of copying whole sections of reference materials into their

research papers, or alternatively, entirely omitting key points. In essence, Think Alouds and subsequent follow-up activities enable Leslie's students to gradually become more metacognitive, or self-aware of their own reading and writing processes.

Throughout the research paper assignment, Leslie also provides class time for students to work on various sections of the paper. During these sessions she circulates around the room and provides individual guidance.

Leslie also teaches note-taking and outlining skills through regular classwork. For example, she has adapted several notetaking strategies involving notebook columns. When students are reading *Julius Caesar* they divide their spiral notebook page into two columns. On the left, they write the scene number, the line number and a general plot statement. Then, as the class discusses what's happening in the play, students take notes on the right. Leslie also uses an adaptation of this method for narrative literature such as *Watership Down* (Adams, 1972) or *Grendel* (Gardner, 1971). The students divide their paper into four columns. The first column is used for facts that students note while reading such as plot, names of characters, and the sequence in which things occur in the text. The second column is reserved for quotes or interesting ideas that students have while reading, and the third is for questions they have while reading. The fourth column is reserved for students to write answers to their questions. Leslie notes that if students come across the answers as they are reading, they can write this down in column 4; if not, they wait until the class discussion and share their questions with other class members (see Figure 7-2).

Throughout every unit Leslie assesses students' prior knowledge, builds background knowledge, and scaffolds new learning in a variety of ways. She also works to facilitate her students' development as reflective readers and writers who can use strategies for improving their own learning. While these are complex goals, Leslie believes they are worth working toward and that they can be accomplished over time.

Emphasis on Writing

Another major emphasis is writing development. Leslie emphasizes a variety of types of writing so that students can develop high levels of competence in writing for different purposes and audiences. Writing assignments vary from what Leslie calls "traditional"—essays on various topics, research papers, and forms of poetry such as ballads and sonnets—to a variety of writing assignments that encourage a response to literature or are linked to students' particular needs. Leslie helps her students develop as writers by providing scaffolds, or instruction she modifies as students become more independent. For example, after seniors wrote essays related to the theme of "violence" in *Macbeth* (see example, Figure 7-3), with students' permission, she used these essays as examples of essay writing techniques when teaching sophomores. These techniques included ways to write a thesis statement, make transitions between sections, and provide evidence to prove a point.

Similarly, when asking students to respond to literature they are reading, Leslie often gives instructions such as those in Figure 7-4. Notice that these instructions give suggestions with room for personal decision-making.

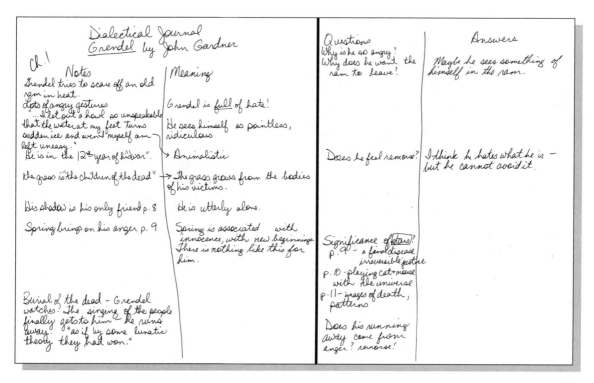

FIGURE 7-2   Student's Four Column Dialectical Journal

Some writing assignments connect directly to students' personal lives and future needs. Writing is also used to build a sense of community in the class. For example, at the beginning of one year Leslie asked students to write "a very short, 100 word autobiographical note, a poem about themselves, and captions for five pictures." Students got to know one another by sharing this writing. The pictures represented events in students' lives "that made them who they are." Another year she began the school year in a similar way, but later turned the assignment into an "autobiographical notebook." Leslie explained that this notebook took form as the year went along and turned out to be "a big notebook with student pictures and writing samples." As a follow-up at the end of the year, Leslie had students write letters to themselves that she planned to mail back to them five years later. As Leslie explains: "I want them to see five years from now where they were. I thought that would make a nice circle: [To] start off with themselves and end with themselves."

Leslie also focuses heavily in her classes on writing that assists students in transitioning to adulthood. For example, she always has seniors write resumes. She finds that this particular activity has great appeal for her students, who see the practical value of the assignment and also use it as an opportunity for thinking about their own goals and past experiences.

FIGURE 7-3   Student's Essay on Violence in *Macbeth*

History has proven that when a violent act is committed the result is more violence. Violent acts, such as murder, war, and suspicion of something done wrong, all result in more violence. In Shakespeare's play *Macbeth* illustrates violence leading to more violence perfectly.

In the world, past and present, murders have been committed at an extraordinary rate. When a murder is committed, there is a high chance that someone will witness the crime. The murderer then knows that if the witness is not dealt with, he will go to the police. The murder has no second thoughts about killing someone else in order to protect himself. This example shows how the violent acts of murder lead to more violence. This is also shown in *Macbeth* when Macbeth kills Banquo after killing Duncan. He does this because Banquo is suspicious of him.

Besides murder causing more violence, the premise of war causes more violence. If one country attacks another country, the original country will then be attacked also. The act of war shows violence begetting more violence. This is also shown in *Macbeth* when war is started because of Macbeth's acts.

Other than murder and war, mere suspicion of someone can cause more violence. One person can do something wrong, and another person becomes suspicious. The first person, in order to save himself, then commits more violent acts, either directly at the second person or at the second's family. This act of violence leading to more violence is also shown in *Macbeth*. Macbeth has Macduff's family murdered, because Macduff is suspicious of Macbeth.

People need to take into perspective that violence does lead to more violence. All the acts of murder, war, and mere suspicion need to be taken care of before tradgedy occurs. Shakespeare's *Macbeth* shows how violence leads to more violence and ending in tragedy.

Modifications for Special Needs

Leslie finds that her curricular emphasis on choice, scaffolding, and strategy instruction is generally well suited to the needs of a diverse population. Students with varying academic needs can usually meet with success in her flexible, supportive environment. Students who have special education needs have Individual Educational Plans (IEP) and support from the special education department at her school. Leslie collaborates with these teachers, and often makes notes in her planbook to remind herself to provide the required support. Often these modifications are simple changes, such as extra time, instructions with fewer steps, or additional use of reading strategies.

SPECIAL PROJECTS AND ASSIGNMENTS

Leslie uses several projects to give students more opportunities for linking reading, writing, and other forms of communication. These longer assignments also enable her to connect her subject area with other disciplines.

English 4
Response Journals

General Description:

Response journals are, just as they sound, your personal response to what you read. They are your opportunity to put your thoughts in writing, to think deeply and to reflect on what you read, on yourself, on our society, the world, its problems, and its successes.

Content:

In your response journal, you should prove to me that you have READ, UNDERSTOOD, AND THOUGHT ABOUT the reading assignment. You can do this in several ways:

1) OUTLINE THE PLOT. The simplest (and least effective) way is to briefly outline the plot. This should take only a couple of sentences and should not, by any means, constitute the whole of the journal.

2) ASK QUESTIONS. Ask questions about something you did not understand and <u>attempt to answer them</u>.

3) CHALLENGE THE AUTHOR. Do you think something the author wrote could have been written better? Differently? If so, bring it up in your journal and discuss it.

4) RELATE IT TO YOUR OWN LIFE. What would you have done if you were in the character's situation? Have you experienced anything similar? If so, describe it.

5) RELATE IT TO THE WORLD. Is there anything in our society that seems similar to or different from what you read in the text? Is there anything right about our society? Anything wrong with it? How can it be corrected?

6) SPECIFIC ASSIGNMENTS. Occasionally I will assign specific assignments for a particular chapter, such as a diary entry, letter, etc.

Use any combination of the above, or make up your own. Just be sure that you are doing your own thinking about your own reading!

FIGURE 7-4   Instructions for Response Journal

One project for sophomores involved reading the novel *Watership Down* (Adams, 1972), writing children's stories based on portions of the book in collaborative small groups, and presenting these to the class and to children at an elementary school. Many groups added dramatic elements or puppetry to their presentations. When discussing the value of the project, Leslie noted the assignment "required students to reword a selection in a story form so that young children would be able to understand and enjoy it." She noted that this translation process provided "a real purpose for rereading, reworking, and rewriting because there was a real audience outside of the high school English classroom."

One hallmark of projects in Leslie's classroom is that they usually provide students with substantial choice, which she believes is strongly linked to motivation. She notes: "Often I let [students] choose what kind of project they want to do. I'll give them a long list of choices and also encourage them to think of other things." For example, in a recent mythology unit, some students created board games, while others created character drawings, story depictions, and plays.

Leslie also finds that students' own interests often propel them to explore a topic well beyond class requirements. She calls this a "spark." One sophomore, for example, got so interested during the study of *Julius Caesar* that he read an additional book about Caesar's military strategies. Leslie explains,

> First, he read all the way through *Julius Caesar*, weeks before we finished it in class. Then he read the book on military strategies during the time when we were doing the play in class. I don't think that he normally would have been interested in reading about military strategies, but he read the book about military strategies all the way through [because of his interest in Julius Caesar].

To encourage all of her students to read for pleasure, Leslie includes 300 pages of "choice reading" with every six-week unit. Students select any book they wish, and Leslie holds conferences with each student every grading period to discuss their reading and reading goals. Leslie has found that students enjoy selecting their own materials and become more experienced at setting and achieving goals throughout the year.

WORKING AS A PROFESSIONAL

Leslie takes many opportunities to increase her expertise as a teacher, using connections both within and beyond her school. She notes that her teacher colleagues provide essential support and advice, even saying they have shaped her philosophy of teaching. Leslie goes on to explain:

> On my first teaching job I was a total wreck. There was nobody else that I could talk to. [In] my second teaching job in California, I was working next door to a very experienced teacher. She didn't tell me much about what to do or really help me with strategies, but was just there so that I could run over to her and say "Help! I can't control this kid! What can I do?" She was always able to offer some advice or just calm me down so that I could think straight. Seeing other people and getting their ideas, [along with] my own experiences as a student have affected my teaching more than anything else.

At Danville High School, Leslie finds a strong and active support system among her departmental colleagues:

> There's a group of teachers at school [who are] all good friends and bounce ideas off each other all the time. We can take an idea and if we talk about it we can figure out how to adapt that idea to our situation. All of us have different strengths in different areas.

This collegial support system is important for Leslie's level of professional satisfaction. However, she does note that she wants to be sure she is also developing her own confidence as a teacher because "sometimes it's easy to be too dependent [on colleagues]."

Leslie also notes that her principal and supervisors have had a positive influence on her development as a teacher, and sees their role as supportive. She believes that her principal is a good administrator who "trusts me to make sound instructional decisions." She also has looked beyond her school for learning opportunities, as she is active in professional organizations and is taking coursework toward her master's degree.

Leslie's philosophy of *how and when* to implement new ideas is practical. She tries to make gradual changes, rather than "completely overhauling" everything she does at once. When she first came to Danville, Leslie says that she followed a very traditional, textbook-based curriculum. The first year she added the autobiography project. Later she added other types of writing, such as the writer's notebook and having students write children's books. In her fourth year at Danville, she was adding changes to the *Macbeth* unit, including a K-W-L (see the Handbook) and student rewriting and presentation of a scene. She also was becoming very involved with computers as the school gained more technology resources, and was looking forward to using Hyperstudio and the Internet with her classes.

Leslie thinks new teachers should be aware of the "real-life" aspects of learning as a teacher. Trying new ideas involves risks, and teachers must be willing to go through several variations when implementing new strategies. As an example, Leslie explains some difficulty she had the year before when she decided to have students make concept maps (see *Sketch to Stretch* in the Handbook, p. 153) related to literature they were reading. She was discouraged by her initial attempts, but planned to try again in a different way:

> The assignment was to take the main characters of the story and to make a diagram showing relationships. [Students] could use circles, lines, symbols and anything else to make a representation of the characters without actually drawing them. I didn't explain it well, apparently, because they didn't get it. To help them out, I took a short story we had read in the class and gave an illustration of a story map. But, when [the students] got to work on their new maps, everything they did was identical to the sample I had done. That was a total wash. They didn't get it at all. I am going to try it again but I guess I'd better give clearer instructions on how to do it.

As a result of this experience, Leslie decided to modify her instruction. Next time she plans to start off by showing students several different concept maps and help them think through different ways they could create their own.

CONCERNS

Leslie's concerns center mainly around the real-life needs of her students. She is especially worried about student drug and alcohol abuse, promiscuity, and issues faced by teenage parents. While she says she doesn't know how to solve these problems, Leslie tries to make her classroom a welcoming place. She does a lot of listening and has learned to speak to students about tough issues to get them thinking. She also encourages students to speak to school counselors and other adults.

In her teaching, Leslie tries to support students by "grabbing the teachable moment" but admits this often is not easy. For example, she regrets that during her first year at Danville a senior came into class with "KKK and a big Swastika on his notebook" and that she failed to say anything because she thought it might cause a conflict. Looking back, she wishes that she had pulled the student aside to discuss what the symbols meant and why they were offensive to others. Leslie believes that teenagers often will follow along with the prejudices of others, but that change is possible if teachers help them understand important concepts and issues.

One major goal that Leslie has is to teach students to treat one another with respect, regardless of financial circumstances, athletic ability, academic success, or other characteristics. She strives to maintain a classroom where students work hard, but also feel safe and will "come and talk to [her] if they need to." She notes that she now grabs those teachable moments, and gives the following example:

> Someone said that a black person could be racist and a lot of kids said, "No!" I said, "Well, I think everybody is racist." Everybody said, "Oh, I am not!" So we started talking about how we could be raised a certain way but a time comes when you have to be responsible for your own thinking. I want my students to be aware that they are ultimately responsible for the way they act. I think at least I can make them aware that they need to be aware.

Overall, Leslie greatly enjoys working with high school students and finds it very satisfying to "to see the way they change, to see them growing up, and be a part of it." She enjoys having the opportunity to introduce her students to new ideas that can help them to grow into "thinking members" of society.

▬ SUMMING UP

In summing up her philosophy of teaching, Leslie talked about imagination. She wants her students to experience literature, mythology, and cultures in her English courses to build their backgrounds and expand their ability to imagine possibilities. As Leslie puts it, "Knowing something about the past makes students deeper people. If all they have in life is going to work, coming home, cooking supper, and going to bed, they never experience . . . imagination, [but] if they can read something and picture it in their heads, then they have a depth to their lives that otherwise wouldn't be there."

Through teaching literature and writing, Leslie finds many opportunities to help her students develop imagination, grapple with new ideas, and build toward the future. It is clear that Leslie greatly enjoys her work and her students, as she says that helping adolescents grow is what "keeps her going."

- After reading this chapter, consider the following questions.
  1. What did you find most interesting or surprising when reading this case?
  2. Look back at your answers to the Thought Questions at the beginning of the chapter. How do you think that Leslie describes teaching English? How is her description similar to or different from yours?
  3. In your own teaching situation, or one with which you are familiar, would it be possible to teach this way? Why or why not?
  4. Leslie included a variety of reading, writing, and oral communication strategies in her instruction. If she wanted to increase her use of literacy even further, what else would you recommend to her?
  5. If you used the *Your Own Questions Strategy*, compare your answers with someone in your class or study group. What are the similarities and differences?

- You may wish to use a content area literacy strategy to reflect on this case study. We suggest *Discussion Web* (see the description in the Handbook, p. 134).

chapter 8

English for Speakers of Other Languages

Mark is a teacher who travels a lot. As one of four teachers responsible for English for Speakers of Other Languages (ESOL) instruction in a rural Virginia county-wide district with 20 schools, Mark is assigned to teach at one elementary, middle, and high school each day. Mark's district, located about halfway between Washington, D.C., and Richmond, Virginia, serves students from a variety of backgrounds. The community is a mix of farm families, small business owners, professionals who work in urban centers, and military families connected with the

nearby Quantico Marine Base. Increasingly, the region is becoming more diverse in terms of the language and cultural background of the students, which has necessitated greater attention to the needs of language minority students.

Mark's students over the past few years have included young people from Latin America, Puerto Rico, China, Russia, Eastern Europe, Vietnam, and the Middle East. He notes that some families immigrated first to large cities such as New York or Washington, D.C., but then moved or sent their children to live with relatives in his district due to concerns about crime and the attraction of gangs in urban areas. Many families are separated, with one or both parents remaining temporarily either in their home country or in an urban area for work. Mark's students also have widely diverse educational backgrounds. While some have had substantial education in their home countries before entering the U.S., others may have attended school irregularly due to war or other disruptions.

Each day, Mark spends about an hour and a half at an elementary building and the same amount of time at a middle school building. He then goes to the high school where he meets for two forty-five minute periods with classes of students that are mixed in grades 9–12. In all three settings he also confers with the other teachers of his students to assist in transitions between mainstream and ESOL classrooms.

Mark's daily travel situation can make his job challenging. However, he finds that serving students at several schools gives him a unique perspective since he often teaches all the children in a family for several years. Mark makes numerous efforts to connect with families beyond the school doors, which enhances his ability to meet the needs of students in the classroom. On weekends or in the evenings, for example, he might be found stopping by a middle school student's birthday party, visiting a family-owned restaurant to talk with a student's uncle about the impact of her work schedule on her school success, or huddled over a kitchen table helping parents with college financial aid forms. Mark believes that developing a positive relationship with students and their families over time helps him assist individuals with problems that could interfere with success in school.

MEETING MARK

Mark was in his fourteenth year of teaching when we first met him and had been working in his current position for six years. Previously, Mark had held a teaching position in a nearby district for six years and also taught for two years in Europe.

When asked about his early background and reasons for becoming a teacher, Mark explained that when he was growing up, his father had worked for the U. S. government in positions that required frequent moves and time abroad. During his childhood and young adult years he lived in Japan, England, Sweden, and Spain, as well as California and Virginia. Mark believes that these experiences encouraged his interest in other cultures and languages and also enabled him to understand what it feels like to be the "new kid" in class and to adjust to different school and home languages.

As a young adult, Mark received a bachelor's degree in English from Occidental College in Los Angeles and then moved to England to teach English as a Foreign Language (EFL) to German students. From there he moved to Spain to teach EFL classes for a year at a language academy. He notes that this experience gave him an understanding of both the positive and negative feelings involved with immersion in a new culture: "When I lived in Spain I was the outsider . . . I learned [Spanish] as I was working and socializing. I never learned it from a textbook."

After returning to the United States, Mark decided to continue his teaching career but realized he would need a teaching certificate. He took courses leading to Virginia teacher licensure at Mary Washington College in Fredericksburg. Mark then accepted a position as the first ESOL teacher in a nearby district, where he was at first employed part-time and had only one student. He later transferred to a full-time middle school position, where he taught a variety of subjects including environmental education and regular English, in addition to ESOL. Mark now says that the experience of teaching both mainstream and ESOL classes was very valuable, as he is able to bring his knowledge from teaching in the content areas into his ESOL teaching:

> I think all this has made me a better ESOL teacher, because by teaching regular classes, I know what the mainstream teacher is faced with. And I know what it does to the mainstream teacher to have an ESOL kid. I realize the impact, the demands on the teacher of having a learner who is so needy. . . . I know how to collaborate in a way that doesn't offend them.

Mark also believes that he gained important knowledge about teaching writing from his work in the middle school environment because his district was moving to a process-based approach:

> A very important part of my training was [teaching in the] middle school . . . that's where I was exposed to the writing process—teaching the writing process. . . . I was suddenly looking at . . . sixth grade teachers, seventh grade teachers . . . observing a lot of what was going on.

Mark later decided to attend George Mason University, about forty-five miles away, to complete a master's degree in Bilingual/Multicultural Education. He then moved into the position he currently holds.

INSIDE MARK'S CLASSROOMS

Mark's classes are small, with between five and twelve students at one time. Generally a class includes all of the English language learners at a school site, except for the high school group, which is divided into two sections based on student schedules. Mark believes small classes are extremely important to his teaching because his students speak a variety of first languages and are vastly different in their levels of English proficiency. Students are also mixed by age and grade level, so their content learning needs are different.

To serve the needs of his diverse groups, Mark has developed a system or framework for teaching in which he plans lessons around themes or topics. He explains that each theme is broad enough to include all students, and that he tailors specific assignments within a lesson to individuals, based upon individual needs and goals. In this way, all students in a class can share common assignments and work together even though their levels of English proficiency may be dramatically different. Mark explains:

> I know what their [individual] needs are, and I direct the instruction at that level. [For example], they're all working on the same topic, and they are all thinking about the same theme. But each one's individual performance level and the skills each one is working on vary.

Collaboration between students is also an important part of the learning atmosphere in Mark's classroom. Students often are together in ESOL classes over several years, so they come to know each other well. Mark facilitates positive interactions by including assignments that help students understand one another. For example, he often starts the year with a writing project entitled, "Who's In ESOL Class?" in which students interview each other and then write biographical sketches (see Figure 8-1). These sketches are used for a class book that is read by everyone in the class.

Another issue that is important to Mark is his own ability to discern the concerns and needs of students whose language and culture may be different from his own and from others in the class. He notes that while he does have a basic knowledge of several languages, his class is conducted in English because the students

FIGURE 8-1 Huei Ping's Biographical Sketch, Written by Marta

Huei Ping

A little beog about Huei Ping. She have name Huei Ping. She is from China and speaks Chinese language. English language she now too (very good) and now she study Spanish language. She came to America 12 years old and now she have 15 years old. She don't have boyfriend but she have friends from China. When she have free time she a sleeping or watch T.V. She don't like to read books because she tnk it too bored. And she don't have a dog or a cat because don't like animals. She liked rock-music, plays basketball, and swimming. And she like cake that have fruit on top.

have different first languages. Mark believes that a good ESOL teacher must be extremely observant of student behaviors and develop "intuition" because students from different cultures may express their feelings with different non-verbal behaviors or verbal intonations and inflections. These subtleties can cause misunderstanding among students from different backgrounds, or between students and the teacher.

Mark notes that he must observe students carefully to interpret their body language and tone of voice in order to understand the feelings they are trying to express and to clear up misunderstandings. For example, one morning when we observed Mark's high school class, he noticed that one young woman was apparently angry with the others. He quietly said something to her and learned that earlier that morning she had thought one of the other students was going to drive her to school. The other student never picked her up because of a miscommunication. Mark was able to help the students resolve this misunderstanding, which was important to their ability to work together within the small classroom community.

Overall, in his teaching Mark is continually looking for ways to encourage his students to use oral and written English to communicate and learn. He finds that building understanding among students from different cultures as well as developing interesting, relevant assignments are central to this goal.

A CLOSE LOOK AT INSTRUCTION

Mark's goals for instruction for his middle and high school students include supporting their development as users of language as well as encouraging learning of concepts that will support their success in content classes. He works to immerse his students in language activities they will find interesting and relevant in order to build communication skills and develop background knowledge on a wide variety of topics. Every unit or theme includes an interconnected set of reading, writing, and discussion opportunities.

Mark says that he enjoys substantial flexibility in his curriculum because his district supervisors recognize that he must meet the multiple needs of diverse students.

He frames his curriculum according to themes (such as the "world of work") that are broad and relevant to any teenager. Within a theme, he uses a very wide variety of reading materials and writing assignments.

On a typical Monday, Mark's students enter his classroom and sit in desks he has arranged in a circle. He begins the class by asking questions about what may have happened over the weekend, both in the local area and in the national or international news. He encourages students to ask questions of one another and of him. This activity facilitates both oral language communication as well as the feeling of community within the class. Often, Mark will then provide a newspaper article for students to read related to a news item or the current unit theme.

Next, Mark turns the students' attention to their current writing project. This may be a new journal entry or a revision of something written earlier. Journal topics often are related to particular units the class is studying. Sometimes Mark also asks students to write on themes such as "fairness," "responsibility," and "honesty" that are part of his school district's word-of-the-month character education program.

Mark finds that through their journal writing, his students build writing fluency and develop ideas they can use for extended writing projects. Mark often writes written replies to students' writing within the journal, so that the journal becomes a dialogue between student and teacher. He says he never corrects or edits student work at this stage, because journal writing is always first-draft writing. However, Mark encourages students to select entries in the journal to expand into work that will be revised, edited, and shared with others.

When students select drafts of their writing to revise, Mark generally is able to take the class to the school's computer lab so they can word process the next draft. He finds the computer labs in his district are available at least once per week for his classes. Mark explains that his students are often more motivated to revise and edit their writing when they are writing on a computer rather than by hand.

After students have created and printed their new draft, Mark holds a conference with each student about their writing in which they discuss both the content ("Can you tell me more about this?") and ways to enhance the clarity of their writing. Students usually revise at least once more, and then do a final copy after Mark has suggested editing changes, including modifications in grammar and spelling. Mark says that while he first emphasizes the content of students' writing, he also wants to be sure that students gradually increase their competence with English mechanics. He teaches students editing symbols and uses these on papers that are ready for the final draft.

Occasionally Mark teaches mini-lessons related to writing, and emphasizes a particular skill for a week or two. For example, Mark mentions that through informal observations he learned that none of his students were using paragraphs appropriately in their writing, so he focused on this skill in a mini-lesson and also in helping students revise their individual work.

Linking Writing, Reading, and Personal History

Mark also uses writing assignments to lead into reading assignments. Throughout the semester, for example, students make class books such as "Who Is In ESOL

Class?," mentioned earlier. Examples of topics that have been made into whole-class books include "Our First Jobs," "Coming to America," and "History We Have Lived." After Mark prints copies of the book for each student to use, he also creates questions and study guides students can use when they are reading one another's work.

When developing "Our First Jobs," students first participated in discussion about the types of jobs they or their friends have had. Then they drafted paragraphs telling about their first jobs. Mark knew from previous conversations that all of the students had worked at some type of job, either within or outside of their own families. Mark participated by asking Maritza to interview him about his first job while the class observed. Maritza summarized the interview and shared it with the class. Later, all students participated as interviewees and interviewers (see Figure 8-2).

Later in the semester, students created another book called "History We Have Lived." Mark explained that the idea for this project came from a newspaper that had a column with a similar title. Although Mark was sure that his students could write similar stories based on their own experiences, he found that students rejected the idea at first, saying they had "not lived through any history." Mark mentioned that his own personal knowledge of each student's past was vital at this point, because he could point out events in their countries that he thought they might remember. With this probing as well as looking at Internet resources related to world events, students soon discovered they knew a lot about many different world events.

Students then began drafting their ideas and sharing with one another. Many students interviewed parents or family members to get more information about an event in their home country. After several rounds of editing and revision, the students compiled the stories into a booklet entitled, "History We Have Lived Through." Yelena's story, "Independence in the Ukraine," went through four drafts before inclusion. Draft 1 (see Figure 8-3) was written in response to a homework assignment, and Mark's comments (top) are primarily content-related (e.g., "What

FIGURE 8-2   Two Excerpts From the Class Book "My First Job"

Mr. C's First Job

Mr. C. decided to take his first job because he likes to swim a lot. He was 13 years old when he got his first job as a gatekeeper at Urbanna Swimming Pool. He got this job because his brother was working as a life guard there.

He had to sign in members and guests and collect money. He had this job for only one summer. He liked the job because it made him feel important. He also liked the job because he could read magazines and get a sun tan. He said that he liked his job because he met different people. He could talk with new people.

In his job he got $2.40 per hour and it was enough for him. Some of that money he put I the bank, the other half he spent on clothes. To get to work he had to ride a bike which was good for him because he didn't have to spend money for gas.

In his free time he swam and played ping pong with his brothers or friends. He could read a book, listen to music, or stay and watch the people who swam in the pool. He could also go out with his friends and have fun.

While he was working he had a lot of fun at work; he just talked to girls and asked for their phone numbers. He also played cards with them to help the time go by. One day he decided to quit this job because he had to go to school and start doing his homework. He didn't have time to work anymore.

By: Maritza

Victor's First Job

Victor's first job was to work at King's dominion, where he still works today. He just started two or three months ago. He drives to work every weekends. He works 18 hours a week at Vitoria's Pizza Restaurant.

He was very busy on his first day, he served drinks and cut pizza on the first day of his job.

He says that he likes his job even though he thinks he won't stay long working there. The thing he likes about his job is that, first, people are very friendly; they help each other at work.

The managers did their job very well. For a new employee like Victor, it only took him two days to get used to his job. They trained Victor enough on what he is supposed to do. He is also satisfied with how much he makes each hour, $6.40 an hour.

Victor thinks that he may not work at Kings Dominion for a long time. He may work somewhere else stable.

By: Eduardo

FIGURE 8-3 First Page of Yelena's First Draft With Mark's Comments

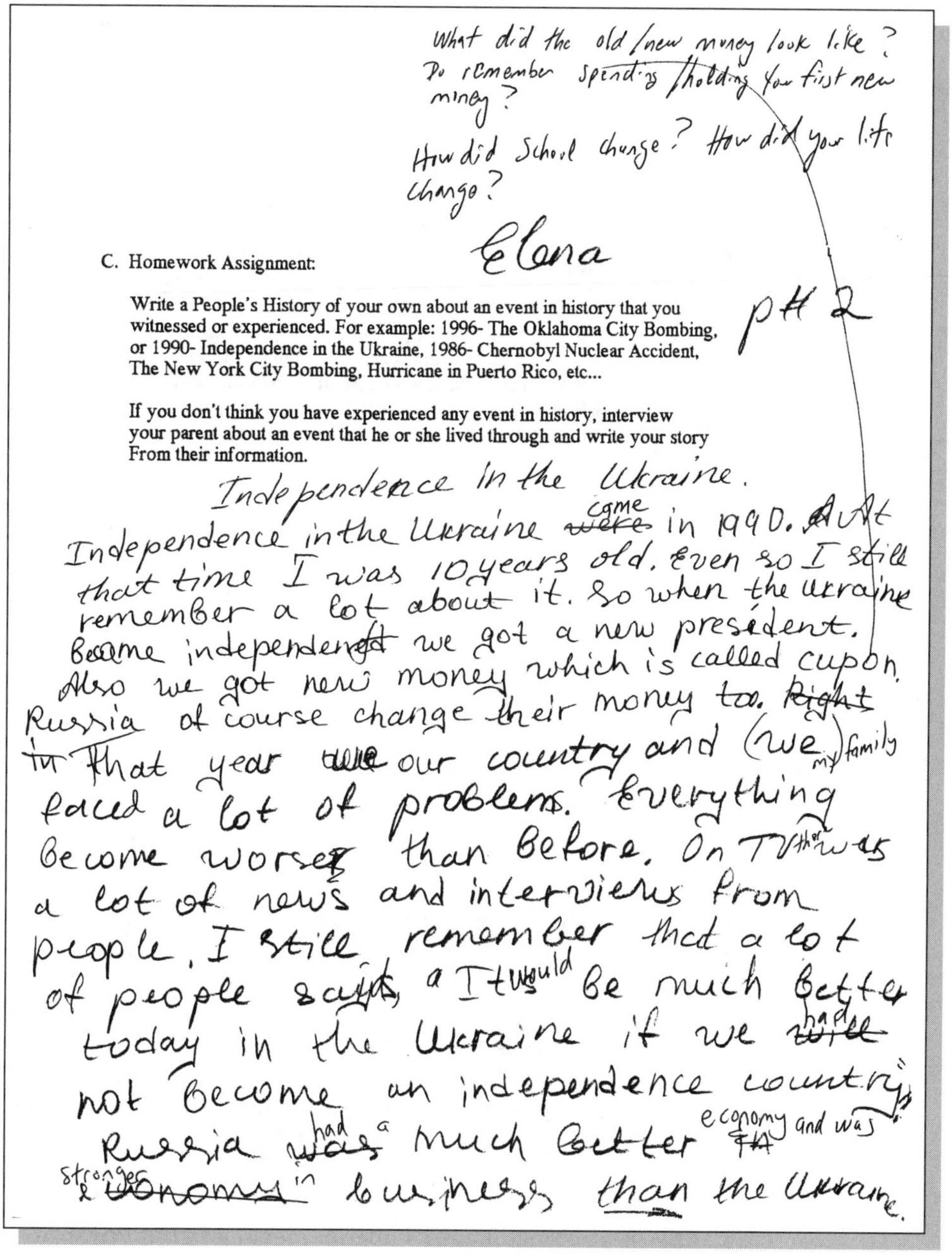

What did the old/new money look like?
Do remember spending/holding your first new
money?

How did School change? How did your life
change?

Elena

C. Homework Assignment:

pH 2

Write a People's History of your own about an event in history that you
witnessed or experienced. For example: 1996- The Oklahoma City Bombing,
or 1990- Independence in the Ukraine, 1986- Chernobyl Nuclear Accident,
The New York City Bombing, Hurricane in Puerto Rico, etc...

If you don't think you have experienced any event in history, interview
your parent about an event that he or she lived through and write your story
From their information.

Independence In the Ukraine.

Independence in the Ukraine ~~were~~ come in 1990. At
that time I was 10 years old. Even so I still
remember a lot about it. So when the Ukraine
Became independent we got a new president.
Also we got new money which is called cupon.
Russia of course change their money too. Right
in that year ~~all~~ our country and (we) my family
faced a lot of problems. Everything
Become worse than Before. On TV there was
a lot of news and interviews from
people. I still remember that a lot
of people said, "It would be much Better
today in the Ukraine if we had
not Become an independence country.
Russia had a much Better economy and was
stronger in business" than the Ukraine.

FIGURE 8-4   First Page of Yelena's Second Draft With Mark's Comments

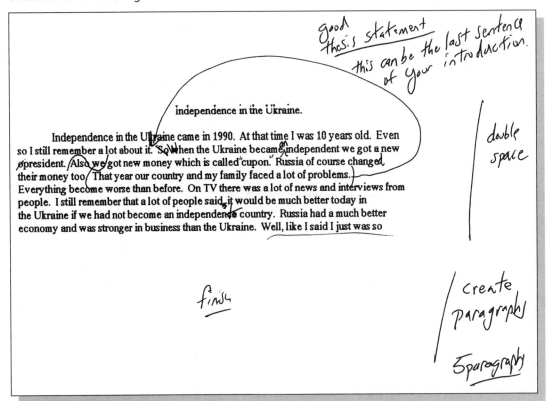

did the old/new money look like?"). For Draft 2 (see Figure 8-4), Yelena used a word processor, and Mark made notes primarily related to the structure of the essay (e.g., "Create paragraphs"). Draft 3 (see Figure 8-5) is an expanded version of Draft 2, in which Yelena has added more detail. Later, Yelena made her final copy for the class book after Mark assisted her with final editing.

When the class books are published, Mark makes copies for all students and also includes some questions to guide their reading. For example, the "World of Work" book included "Who's Who at Work" (Figure 8-6) which required students to read each essay carefully. In the process, they learned a great deal about their classmates.

Mark also encourages students' personal connection to published reading materials. For example, he mentions that his students responded in a highly positive way to the novel *The Journey of the Sparrows* (Buss & Cubias, 1991) about young people who sneak into the United States without appropriate legal documents. Mark explained that this book struck a chord with his students because it was "so

FIGURE 8-5   First Page of Yelena's Final Draft

Yelena

INDEPENDENCE IN THE UKRAINE

Independence in the Ukraine came in 1990. At that time I was 10 years old. Even so I still remember a lot about it. That year our country and my family faced a lot of problems. Everything become worse than before. When the Ukraine became independent we got a new president and new money which is called coupon. On TV there was a lot of news and interviews from people. I still remember that a lot of people said, it would be much better today in the Ukraine if we had not become an independent country. Russia had a much better economy and was stronger in business than the Ukraine. Well, like I said I just was too young to understand what is really going on in my country.

Schools didn't really changed a lot. And nobody talked about it in school. Exsually it happened in summer time. I was in county side when I first heard and saw this news and money.

People in country side really didn't worry much about future of the Ukraine and what is going on in government and city. Well, anyway I just remember the other day I was buying a

---

much about them" and that it led to a lot of conversation, discussion, and ideas. He also mentions that when he lived in Spain as a young adult he did not have legal work papers, so he understands his students' personal issues at a deeply personal level.

Mark's students are also encouraged to bring in reading material from their other classes. For example, one student, Elena, was taking a course in food occupations and shared readings on metabolism and diet with the rest of the class. Mark also notes that materials that address student interest in current fads and health issues have great appeal. For example, he says that when "everyone was getting pierced" he found a book on the topic and shared it with the class.

Overall, while the topics Mark's students read and write about are clearly wide-ranging, his instruction is always focused on improving their reading, writing, and language development. Students work both individually and together as they work toward greater understanding of their own histories and issues in their new country.

FIGURE 8-6   "Who's Who At Work" Class Assignment

Who's Who At Work

Write the name of the person:

Learned the job quickly in just two days   _____
Had a manager who was from the same country   _____
Felt tired and never had time for homework   _____
Was nervous during the interview   _____
Played cards while at work   _____
Doesn't think that $6.40 an hour is a great wage   _____
Worked without getting paid   _____
Won an award for being a valuable employee   _____
Thinks that the people at work are friendly   _____
Didn't like to see the food go to waste   _____
Worked to help out family   _____
Swam during breaks   _____
Rode the roller coaster after work   _____
Started work at the age of twelve   _____
First pay check in the bank   _____
Put "Likes to talk to people and meet people at work" _____
Doesn't plan to stay in this job a long time   _____

Special Projects and Assignments

Throughout the year, Mark watches closely for assignments that really catch his students' interest and turns a few of these into major projects. For example, one year several students became interested in a book of games they found in the school library. Mark encouraged others to read sections of the book, primarily to help them to learn to follow written directions in English. Eventually, however, students started to teach one another a variety of games, and the idea of teaching games at the district's Multicultural Day emerged.

Multicultural Day is a district-wide event, sponsored by ESOL and foreign language teachers in the district, in which a full Saturday is spent celebrating languages and cultures. People throughout the community are involved, including businesses, vendors, speakers, musicians, and artists. High schools within the county sponsored booths of various types. Mark's students decided to run booths with games from different cultures. It was the students' responsibility to research the origin of a game and learn its rules. They then created the materials necessary to play the game as well as a poster that explained the rules. Students were able to choose games from their own culture, or from a different culture. During class, Mark used a variety of strategies to help students learn background information about the games they had selected. For example, students created charts to compare features of various games and used the Internet to look up information on the country in which various games had originated.

During the preparation period and Multicultural Day itself, students continually used a wide variety of language skills to learn about the games and communicate with others. They also used mathematics to understand scoring systems and artistic abilities in poster preparation. In addition, individuals and the group established important ties to other students in their school as well as members of the community.

Mark also has begun to develop special projects using technology. His students often communicate through email, even sending homework to him through this medium. In the future, he plans to have his students create their own website. He explains that this will allow his students to communicate with other ESOL students across the country who share the same types of concerns. Increased use of technology will also be a way he can teach his students computer skills that will help them in the workplace.

WORKING AS A PROFESSIONAL

Mark is always looking for ways to improve his teaching and his understanding of his students. He collaborates extensively both within his school and with other teachers he meets in the district or over the Internet. At the middle and high school he is responsible for assisting his students in their content area courses. He often administers quizzes and tests and helps students with content assignments that require a lot of reading and writing. Sometimes he helps content teachers make modifications to tests, such as question format or response mode, so that they can more accurately evaluate a student's learning. Mark also tries to be a voice for his students when they have concerns or problems in their regular classes. He finds that many times his students are uncomfortable asking questions in front of a large group, or are unable to express their needs to their content area teachers.

Mark also provides training for content area teachers. Twice a year he and the other ESOL teachers in his district conduct workshops for all of the teachers in the district. The workshops attempt to provide content area teachers with resources and strategies to understand and accommodate the needs of ESOL students. He wrote his district's training manual for content area teachers who work with ESOL students.

Looking beyond his own school district, Mark also has a strong commitment to learning from and with teachers across the country. He frequently uses email listserves and websites established for ESOL teachers (for example, see www.davesesolcafe.com). He feels this on-line exchange is crucial to staying current in the field, especially since in many regions, ESOL teachers are isolated from one another and do not have the opportunity to collaborate. As he notes: "Because of the computer, the ESOL teacher is no longer working in isolation. You can be teaching ESOL in the middle of Kansas and have only five ESOL kids and have access to what's going on."

Another way Mark is able to collaborate with other ESOL teachers is by being a member of professional organizations at both the local and national levels. Mark attends the yearly conferences of several organizations and often presents workshops. He finds the opportunities for professional development invaluable.

CONCERNS

Mark explained that his biggest concern is helping his students successfully adjust to life in the United States. His goal is to serve as a bridge, so that students can build an understanding of a new language and a new culture, while still holding onto the beliefs and traditions they bring with them. He also notes that as adolescents, his high school students often have difficulty related to "fitting in," which causes stress:

> . . . Being so different . . . standing out by race, by language, by culture. They have a hard time making friends in such a homogenous school in a suburb . . . many are really shy . . . they are facing more than the average teenager. Layer on top of that questions of identity and race and language and acceptance . . . what your parents expect versus what works in school and what's going on in society . . . that creates a lot of stress in these kids.

Mark also notes that many of his students who arrive in the United States in middle or high school face more difficulty than students who arrive at younger ages. They often have moved many times, have lived in stressful situations, have had limited education in their home countries, and have endured separations from family. Because they first enroll in U.S. schools during adolescence, they also have a very short time in which to adequately prepare for high school graduation. Mark notes that research he has studied indicates that ". . . it takes five to seven years for [students] to catch up academically . . . [especially in] the higher level thinking, organization, and analysis in writing . . . ." Students arriving at age 13 or older therefore face a daunting task to develop the language and content knowledge necessary for passing high school courses and state competency tests. Mark works closely with individual students to help them achieve success, and also suggests alternatives to traditional high school when appropriate.

While most of his students gradually overcome their difficulties, a few have responded to stress by running away from home, getting into legal trouble, or dropping out of school. Often, however, these students return to try again. Mark notes that he is very proud that most of his students are working and attending school. Most graduate from high school, and many go on to attend either two year or four-year colleges.

SUMMING UP

Mark is a teacher who clearly enjoys his diverse group of students and works tirelessly to meet their needs. A hallmark of his instruction is his creative effort to develop appropriate instruction for his students that connects to their backgrounds, needs, and interests. He also has developed strong connections with his students and their families through his work within and beyond the school. Mark's efforts enable his students to develop English language and literacy skills while gaining new understandings and connections that will assist them as they move toward adulthood.

- After reading this chapter, consider the following questions.
  1. What did you find most interesting or surprising when reading this case?
  2. Look back at your answers to the Thought Questions at the beginning of the chapter. How do you think Mark describes teaching ESOL? How is his description similar to or different from yours?
  3. In your own teaching situation, or one with which you are familiar, would it be possible to teach this way? Why or why not?
  4. Mark included a variety of reading, writing, and oral communication strategies in his instruction. If he wanted to increase his use of literacy even further, what else would you recommend to him?
  5. If you used the *Directed Reading-Thinking Activity*, share your initial predictions and what you confirmed, refined, or eliminated with someone in your class or study group. What are the similarities and differences?

- You may wish to use a content area literacy strategy to reflect on this case study. We suggest *Progressive Writing* (see the description in the Handbook, p. 145).

Reflecting on Teaching and Learning

W hat is the best way to improve content area teaching, learning, and literacy? This question is of great interest to a wide variety of individuals—teachers, students, parents, administrators, employers, and politicians. Each of these stakeholders in the educational process approaches educational improvement from a different perspective. The individual teacher, however, is in a unique position to make decisions that dramatically affect student opportunities for learning on a day-in, day-out basis. In essence, the teacher holds the key position to make a difference.

Your reflection on the case studies that you have just read can have powerful implications. First, by considering these cases in light of your own experiences and knowledge in your content field, you may glean unique insights that will assist you in addressing the needs of your own current or future students. In addition, you can carry your reflections one step further by using them to guide your inquiry as a teacher researcher.

While studying each chapter, you may have tried out some of the strategies designed to help readers improve their comprehension and learning. You also may have used the case analysis chart (Figure 1-1) to record your summaries for aspects of each case. In this chapter, we suggest some additional ways to continue your inquiry into content area literacy. First, we suggest that you conduct a cross-case comparison of the cases in the book to consider how the teachers are similar or different in their approaches to instruction and content literacy. You can begin this process by using the charts you have already completed, and continue by comparing each teacher's practices with the practices of the others. A suggested format for your comparisons appears in Figure 9-1.

After making your own comparisons, we suggest you share them with others, both in your own and other content areas. What do you, as a group, see as similarities and differences across teachers? How do you think these teachers' practices

FIGURE 9-1 Cross-Case Analysis Format (For Use With Text Chapters)

Nature of Instruction in Case	Grade 6 Social Studies	Grade 7 Team	Grade 8 Social Studies and English	High School Biology	High School Math	High School English	English for Speakers of Other Languages
Approaches to Reading							
Approaches to Writing							
Approaches to Classroom Discussion							
Approaches to Motivation/ Engagement							
Nature of Classroom Organization							
Other Category (Your Choice)							
Other Category (Your Choice)							

compare to recommendations of professional organizations, such as those who have written content area or literacy standards? (Summaries of standards appear in the Content Area Handbook and later in this chapter.)

LOOKING BACK: WHAT ADOLESCENTS DESERVE

You may recall from Chapter 1 that the International Reading Association's Commission on Adolescent Literacy, a collaboration of educators from throughout North America, published a "Position Statement on Adolescent Literacy" (Moore et al., 1999). Each of the seven principles in the statement begins with the phrase "Adolescents deserve . . . " because the emphasis in the statement is on what schools and districts should do to support their adolescent learners.

FIGURE 9-2   Four Supports for Literary Learning

Schools serving young adolescents should provide:

1. Continuous reading instruction for all young adolescents
2. Reading instruction that is individually appropriate
3. Assessment that informs instruction
4. Ample opportunities to read and discuss reading with others

Source: Supporting Young Adolescents' Literacy Learning: A Joint Position Paper of the International Reading Association and the National Middle School Association (2002). Newark, DE: Author. (http://www.reading.org/positions/supporting_young_adolesc.html)

Recently, other organizations and groups of educators concerned about literacy have joined their voices in the effort to place increased emphasis on the literacy needs of adolescents. For example, the National Middle School Association recently collaborated with the International Reading Association in publishing "Supporting Young Adolescents' Literacy Learning: A Joint Position Paper." This position paper offers four essential supports that schools should provide and also issues "A Call for Action" that gives educators, families, and policy-makers guidelines for assisting adolescent literacy learners (see Figure 9-2). The National Reading Conference, an international organization of literacy researchers, also has recently produced important guidelines related to adolescent literacy through its commissioning of a white paper entitled "Effective Literacy Instruction for Adolescents" (see Alvermann, 2002, or www.nrconline.org). All of these documents provide a strong basis for considering the best ways to develop a program for adolescent learners in your own school or district. In addition, they all emphasize the important role content area teachers play when they take specific steps to make a real difference in the literacy, lives, and learning of teenagers.

We suggest that you take a look at one or more of these position statements, as well as the standards in your own discipline (summarized in the Handbook). Consider what you see as key elements found in several documents. Which of these can you envision emphasizing in your own instruction?

LOOKING FORWARD: TEACHING AS INQUIRY

It is our view that all teachers should be focused on inquiry, or action research, in relation to the needs of their students. For example, the curriculum for a particular course can be viewed as the treatment portion of a grand, year-long experiment. At the beginning of the year, a teacher sets a tentative agenda for implementing a variety of interventions. Like a traditional researcher, a teacher pretests or gathers baseline data (assessment), then applies an intervention (instruction), and later gathers data once again to see if any change has occurred.

A teacher, however, has a much more difficult job than a typical empirical researcher as there are numerous and ongoing sources of information which must continually be monitored during a lesson, such as facial expressions, body language, tone of voice, student questions, and student answers. There also are multiple ways of gathering baseline data about students and what they already know. One can very simply administer a pretest, but that is often not an efficient use of teaching time. It may be more efficient to build ongoing opportunities for assessment into your teaching. For example, the K-W-L strategy (Ogle, 1986) gets students actively involved in the proposed area of study. This strategy also provides the teacher an opportunity to see what students already know, what misconceptions they might have, and what gaps exist in their knowledge. By obtaining and reflecting on this information, the teacher is actively collecting data and establishing hypotheses about how to proceed with teaching. Hypotheses may be as simple as saying to oneself that a particular point in the text should be highlighted, or it may be as complex as realizing that the planned lesson will bomb because students do not have enough background knowledge to make connections to what is supposed to be taught. In this case, the teacher might decide to put the lesson on a back burner until some background knowledge is built through watching a video, providing a hands-on experience, and so forth.

We suggested earlier that teacher action research is a powerful means of professional development that puts the teacher in the driver's seat. Mills (2003) agrees that while action research is certainly not a panacea for educational reform, it can make a significant difference in creating a sense of professionalism that "encourag(es) teachers to be continuous learners" (p. 10). Many of the activities suggested in this text can be seen as forms of teacher research, as they encourage inquiry into the teaching process of others or oneself. Moving forward to the next step of teacher research, in which you set your own questions, collect and analyze data, and ponder the results, allows you to guide your own learning through questions that have emerged from your practice.

Figure 9-3 presents a list of steps for the action research process that were developed several years ago by Vacca and Rasinski (1992, p. 267). Teachers can use these as guidelines for developing their own projects.

TAKING A STANCE AS A TEACHER RESEARCHER

In writing this text we have used field notes, videos, interviews, and classroom artifacts to create the cases presented, and have tried to present an accurate picture of each teacher, including their personal characteristics, thoughts, beliefs, practices, and classroom environments. As noted earlier, the cases are of real teachers, not perfect teachers. Our purpose in the creation of these cases was to provide food for thought, discussion, and reflection.

Now that you have read several case studies and conducted a cross-case analysis, you may want to focus specifically on your own content area. First, using the research process steps suggested, develop questions. Then go out and observe one or more teachers in your area of teaching. Collect information that will help answer your questions, but also be open to new questions that emerge during your observations. Talk seriously with educators in your district or region about adolescents' literacy

FIGURE 9-3   Steps in the Action Research Process

- Recognize that there are many questions that need to be addressed and answered in any classroom.
- Focus on a question or set of related questions that, if answered, can have a positive impact on students.
- Develop a workable plan for answering the question. Decide on which methods are best suited to collect data that is related to the question.
- Implement the research plan. Collect relevant information (i.e., data).
- Analyze the data. Try to make sense out of the information collected. Ask, what does this information have to say about the original question.
- Arrive at a conclusion or answer to the question. Use the conclusion to make appropriate changes in the classroom.
- Disseminate the results to others, either informally (through discussion or school staff meetings) or formally (through presentations at professional meetings or publications in professional newsletters or journals).

Source: Vacca, R. T., & Rasinski, T. V. (1992). *Case studies in whole language.* New York: Harcourt Brace Jovanovich College Publishers.

FIGURE 9-4   Format for Instructional Observation

School type/location:
Teacher (use pseudonym):
Date: Time: Subject:
Grade Level: Topic:

1. Classroom Climate:
2. Activities:
3. Teaching Style:
4. Personal Characteristics:
5. Approach to Diversity:
6. Student Motivation:
7. Student Engagement:
8. Classroom Talk:
9. Classroom Organization:
10. Teaching Approaches:
11. Meeting Student Needs:
12. Incorporation of Literacy:
13. Classroom Management:

and learning, and talk with adolescents themselves. After you have collected data, you can compare and contrast aspects of what you observed and heard with information from the cross-case analysis you conducted earlier.

You may use the framework in Figure 9-4 for taking notes regarding a variety of details. You also may want to add your own categories and questions. When you have completed your observations, bring your findings to your class or study group and discuss them with others. Think about how the teachers you observed are similar to and different from the cases in this book. Consider what you want to remember as you make professional decisions and how you can adapt what you have seen to your own situation.

FINAL THOUGHTS

The case studies that have been presented throughout this book are examples of the many types of excellent teaching that exist in schools today. We hope these cases have provided you with food for thought about the central role that content teachers can play in helping adolescents grow in literacy and knowledge. Our purpose has also been to provide you with a variety of tools that can help you meet your goals for your own professional development. You also may want to think about the questions in Figure 9-5 as you consider your next steps as a professional educator.

Adolescents and educators who work with them face enormous challenges. Yet, adolescence is a wonderful age of change and development. Professional educators who take their learners seriously and guide them effectively in developing knowledge, understanding, and multiple forms of literacy can make a real and permanent difference in the lives of young people.

FIGURE 9-5   Framework for Professional Development

My Strengths:

My Challenges:

My Beliefs:

My Goals:

My Plan for Reaching My Goals:

Content Area Handbook

Contents

Teaching and Learning Strategies Referenced in Chapters   131

    Brainstorming   132

    Categorization and Word Maps   132

    Discussion Web   134

    Double Entry Journals   135

    DR-TA or Directed Reading–Thinking Activity   136

    Graphic Organizers (*see* Semantic Mapping)

    INSERT (Interactive Notation System to Effective Reading and Thinking)   138

    K-W-L   139

    LINK (List, Inquire, Note, Know)   141

    Post-Graphic Organizer   142

    Prediction   142

    PreP (Pre Reading Plan)   143

    Progressive Cinquain   144

    Progressive Writing   145

    Save the Last Word for Me   145

    Semantic Mapping and Graphic Organizers for Expository Text Structure   146

      Descriptive Text Structure   148

      Sequential Text Structure   149

      Compare/Contrast Text Structure   150

      Cause/Effect Text Structure   151

      Problem/Solution Text Structure   152

Sketch to Stretch   153

Summarization   153

Think–Pair–Share   154

Webbing (*see* Semantic Mapping)

Word Maps (*see* Categorization)

Your Own Questions   155

References for Teaching and Learning Strategies   155

National Standards and Goals   157

Agriculture   157

English Language Arts   158

ESL   160

Mathematics   160

Science   163

Social Studies   164

Technology   165

Visual Arts   166

Additional Suggestions for Case Analyses and Field Experiences   167

Areas to Consider When Conducting Observations   167

Suggestions for Teacher Interviews   168

Case Analysis Chart   169

Cross Case Analysis Chart   171

Additional Resources and Websites   172

Constructivism and Inquiry Learning   172

Adolescent Literacy and Content Literacy   172

Effective Teaching   172

Professional Organizations   173

Websites by Subject Area   174

References for Teaching With the Internet   175

Teaching and Learning Strategies Referenced in Chapters

If teachers want to develop active, independent learners who can apply a variety of strategies, a substantial amount of time should be spent to develop students' metacognitive abilities (Alvermann & Moore, 1991; Nist & Simpson, 2000; Paris, Wasik, & Turner, 1991). The strategies presented in this section provide insight into declarative, procedural, and conditional knowledge that leads to independent, active learning. However, the teacher employing the strategy must monitor and adjust the strategy according to the specific content area and ability level of the students in the class. When adjusting, the key is to keep the underlying processes in mind so that the teacher can give students feedback on their processing attempts. To help students gain ownership of strategies and transfer these learning processes across content areas, it is critical to have students engage in reflection about what occurred in their heads while employing the strategy, how it affected their learning, and how the process might be applied in other contexts.

The key processes that research has consistently shown to improve older students' learning are: organization, question generation/answer explanation, text summarization, and student generated elaborations (Nist & Simpson, 2000). With the pressure of high stakes testing and time constraints, many content area teachers are understandably hesitant to go beyond the adopted textbook, let go of lecture as a primary teaching method, or give more control to students. However, relying on a teacher-centered transmission approach may not accomplish learning goals beyond surface-level knowledge of content (Wade & Moje, 2000).

The following strategies provide simple frameworks for easily integrating strategies and processes that improve learning and integrate social construction into the content classroom (Bean, 2000). For those teachers who are fearful that students may not be getting the content when these strategies are employed, the authors suggest that the last five to ten minutes of the class period be reserved for "Concept and Process Reflection."

To engage students in concept and process reflection, have students take turns explaining what they learned while the teacher writes their insights on the board or chart paper. After their insights have been recorded, share a transparency with the key concepts you, the content expert, would have covered in a lecture. Have the students compare what they learned with the concepts that you thought were most important by asking, "What ideas on this transparency surprise you? Why?" Typically, most key concepts have already been listed by the students, but this gives the students an opportunity to see if they missed anything important—and it gives the teacher an opportunity to assess students' learning and explain a content expert's thinking as to why something they missed is important.

BRAINSTORMING (Based on Vacca and Vacca, 2002; Vaughan and Estes, 1986)

A before-reading strategy that helps students activate schema in order to maximize comprehension. Brainstorming is a simple way to help students activate prior knowledge before reading. This "What do you think of when I say?" activity is the cornerstone for many of the more sophisticated prereading activities such as clustering, conceptual mapping, or K–W–L. As the teacher records students' responses, assessment of the knowledge base of the students is possible. As the students brainstorm items, the teacher may extend concepts or define terms that the students will encounter when reading the text. Since brainstorming is a flexible strategy that requires marginal manipulation of information, it is particularly useful when students have little prior knowledge of a subject.

CATEGORIZATION AND WORD MAPS (Based on Schwartz, 1988; Schwartz & Raphael, 1985; Vacca and Vacca, 2002)

A before-, during-, or after-reading strategy that helps students determine hierarchical relationships. The basic processes underlying this categorization are analyzing, determining relationships, and organizing. A concept of definition framework will be used to provide an initial structure to use. This activity is the cornerstone for many of the more sophisticated strategies such as graphic organizers, open/closed sorting, concept circles, and concept of definition.

Procedure:

- Select key vocabulary words or technical terms that are important for students to understand related to the topic.
- Provide word maps of a general hierarchical structure (see Exhibits 1 and 2) with key terms inserted.
- Discuss levels of categories and provide examples such as fruit: apple, red delicious; automobile: Ford, Taurus; etc.
- Have students read individually or in pairs and fill in the word map. Clarify that they are to add additional categories that they believe are important as they read.
- After reading, have students share and discuss their word maps in small groups.
- For closure, have groups share their maps with the whole class and facilitate discussion (see Exhibit 3).

If you are using this strategy with Chapter 5 (see Exhibit 3), fill in another coordinate category such as "Content" and then list the subordinate categories you find while reading.

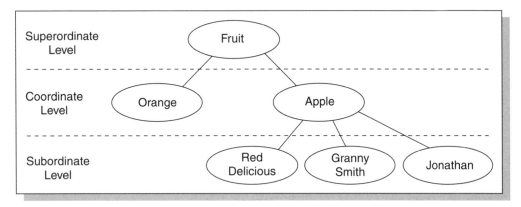

EXHIBIT 1   Levels of Categorization

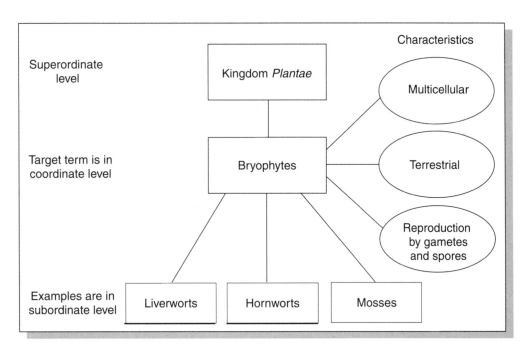

EXHIBIT 2   Concept of Definition Word Map for Bryophytes

Options:

- Provide a list of terms that are important to understanding the topic prior to reading. Have students sort the terms into their own categories (open sort). During or after reading, have students sort the same terms into conceptual categories based on the reading. Have them share and defend their categories by providing support from the text.

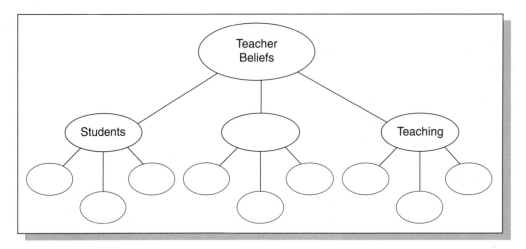

EXHIBIT 3

- Provide a list of terms that are important to understanding the topic prior to reading. Provide superordinate categories into which the terms should be sorted during reading (closed sort). After reading, have students share the way they categorized the terms by citing specific support (page number and paragraph) from the text.
- During reading, have students find the superordinate category, a coordinate category, several properties, and several examples for each key term (see concept of definition word map in Exhibit 2 for an example). After reading, have students extend their connections by encouraging them to provide other coordinate categories, properties, and examples from their reading and new connections to their prior knowledge.

DISCUSSION WEB (Based on Alvermann, 1991)

An after-reading strategy that helps students actively consider alternative points of view regarding an issue before drawing conclusions. The underlying processes include thinking critically, providing evidence to support two points of view, and drawing conclusions. This strategy is particularly useful to stimulate and structure small group discussions.

Procedure:

- Prepare students for reading, listening, or viewing by activating prior knowledge, having students make predictions, brainstorming, asking their own questions, etc.
- Have students read the text, listen to a lecture, or watch a video or demonstration. Taking notes during this phase is helpful.
- Introduce the Discussion Web Format and the Central Question (see Exhibit 4).
- Have students work in pairs to discuss/defend their points of view while writing down their reasons under the "No" and "Yes" columns. Tell students that they are to take turns and allow the same amount of time for responses in each column.

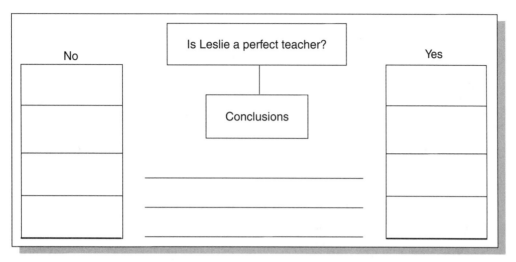

EXHIBIT 4   Discussion Web for Chapter 7

- When all pairs of students have jotted down several reasons in each column, have pairs combine to form groups of four students.
- Have the four students compare the reasons listed on their webs and discuss their views while working toward a conclusion that most can agree with. Total consensus is not necessary as dissenting views can be aired later, but a conclusion must be jotted down.
- Have each group decide which three reasons best support their conclusion and select a spokesperson to present to the whole class.
- Follow up with whole-class discussion and allow students with dissenting opinions to express their views.
- After presentations and discussion, have each student respond to the central question in writing and provide reasons for their conclusion.

DOUBLE ENTRY JOURNALS (Based on Caulkins, 1986)

A during-reading strategy in which students record conceptually-related dual entries in response to a prompt that helps them summarize, react to ideas presented by the author, and reflect on their comprehension processes as they are reading. The underlying processes include self-monitoring of comprehension and developing metacognitive awareness.

Procedure:

- Have students fold a sheet of paper in half from top to bottom.
- At the top of the left column have students write, "What the author says!" At the top of the right column have students write, "What it means to me."
- As students read, have them copy or summarize an important statement, key concept, theory, definition, or text that requires clarification from the text in the left column.

- In the right column, students record their thoughts, questions, or whatever comes to mind as they try to make sense of what was copied.

Options:

- For younger students or those that have not had experience with double entry journals, provide a key word or prompt for the left column that asks about the major concept presented in the text to be read.
- Model double entries on the board, using Think Aloud to guide students who are not familiar with journal response.

DR–TA or DIRECTED READING–THINKING ACTIVITY (Based on Stauffer, 1969; Manzo and Manzo, 1990; Vacca and Vacca, 2002)

A before-, during-, and after-reading strategy that helps students develop purposes for reading, engage in reasoning while reading, affirm their knowledge, and confront their misconceptions. DR–TA is best described as using the scientific method with text, since the key underlying process is hypothesis testing. Students predict based on their prior knowledge and experience, then read to confirm or refute their predictions. This strategy is a powerful teaching tool with both narrative and expository text, but students must have some background knowledge of the topic before it can be used effectively with expository text.

DR–TA Procedure for Narrative Text and Stories:

- Have students predict what the story will be about from the title or illustrations by asking, "What do you think this [story, chapter, section] will be about?" Encourage multiple predictions and write them on the board.
- Go back to the students who gave predictions and ask them, "Why do you think so?" Probe for prior experiences and background knowledge.
- Have students read silently to a logical stopping point that you have predetermined (see Exhibit 5). Have students mask or cover text beyond the stopping point with a sheet of paper.
- As the majority of students come to the stopping point, ask, "What do you think will happen now? Why?" Have them verify their reasoning with support from the text. Write new predictions on the board. Also ask, "Which predictions can we eliminate? Why?" Have students provide supporting information from the text and if the class agrees, draw a line through the prediction on the board.
- Repeat the previous two steps until you get to the last stopping point, then ask, "How do you think this story will end? Why?"
- Have students read to the end of the story, then ask, "Why did the story end this way? How would you have ended the story?"

Title and/or illustration at the beginning of the text.

Introduction to characters, setting, and/or initiating event.

Main character's initial response to the event.

Attempts to solve the problem or achieve a goal.

Consequence or outcome of attempt.

Main character's reaction to consequence or outcome.

EXHIBIT 5   Logical Stopping Points in a Story

Procedure for Informational and Expository Text:

- Set the purpose for reading by having students predict what information the author will present based on a title, subheading, chart, graph, map, etc. Record their hypotheses on the board and ask, "Why do you think so?" Probe for background knowledge and information from prior learning.
- Probe to assess whether students have an adequate knowledge base or if misconceptions and lack of a knowledge base will hinder comprehension of the text. If probing reveals difficulties, discuss prior learning, clarify concepts, and review technical terms to help students create somewhat logical theories. Be aware that this should not become an interrogation that shuts down student risk-taking. Rather, it should be an open-ended discussion that encourages student inquiry, discussion, and development of alternative hypotheses.

- Have students read silently to a logical, predetermined stopping point to see if their hypotheses are correct. Predetermine the stopping points based on the concept/concepts you are attempting to cover and the nature of the text. For example, you may have several paragraphs focused on one concept and only one stopping point at the end of the passage. Or you may have multiple stopping points if the main concept includes several ideas or constructs. If you use multiple stopping points, have students mask or cover text beyond the stopping point with a sheet of paper.
- As the majority of students come to the stopping point, conduct whole class or small group discussions in which students accept, reject, or modify the previously posed hypotheses providing support from the text. If small group discussion is used, have each group appoint a recorder to share the group's thinking with the whole class. Remember to use open-ended questions such as: "How do you know?" and "Why do you think so?" Always have students provide supporting information from the text and if the class agrees, modify the hypotheses on the board.
- Repeat the previous step until you complete the selected passage.

Options:

- Once all predictions or theories have been recorded on the board, a poll can be taken and debate intensified. When completing this strategy with informational or expository text, be sure to have reference materials at hand so that students can support their hypotheses.
- For those students who finish reading more quickly, have them jot down ideas on the blank sheet of paper that they are using to mask the text. For example, they can write down which predictions they think are still correct and why, or create new predictions based on the new information they just finished reading.

INSERT (INTERACTIVE NOTATION SYSTEM TO EFFECTIVE READING AND THINKING) (Based on Vaughan and Estes, 1986)

INSERT is a during-reading strategy that helps readers consciously interact with text to clarify their thinking. INSERT gets readers interacting with the text by "inserting" their thoughts into the ideas proposed by the text to monitor their comprehension and make decisions such as, "I knew that," "I don't understand," and "That's really important." The decisions included in INSERT embody a range of ways in which text can be understood. Since the decisions are conscious and noted, they can be discussed, examined, justified, and modified. These types of decisions provide a basis for critical thinking and reasoning by clarifying what one thinks about the ideas presented in the text.

The decision-making process students engage in is better than underlining for three reasons. First, most students in public schools are not permitted to underline in their books. Second, underlining is often not helpful because developing learners are not clear about what to underline. Third, underlining is not important, but the reason for underlining is important. INSERT makes the reason for the notation immediately apparent at a glance. We consider INSERT an ideal strategy to prepare students for discussion after they read.

Procedure:

Students make **INSERT** notations as shown below during reading. Notations may be made directly in the text, on sticky notes attached to the text, on clear plastic, or on a paper folded into four columns (with the page number written at the top of each column) to help them monitor their comprehension, interact with the text, and consciously make decisions about the ideas in the text.

INSERT Reminder

I agree = ✓	That's new = +	I wonder = ?
I disagree = X	That's important = !	I don't understand = ??

Options:

- Consider introducing this strategy gradually to students based on their developmental level. For example, young or immature readers might only use the "✓" and "x" to start. When they become used to these notations, introduce others.
- Create your own notations, but remember that students must understand when to use notations and why they are using them. The object of INSERT is to get students to monitor their comprehension and critically consider the ideas they find in the text.

K–W–L STRATEGY (Based on Carr and Ogle, 1987; Ogle, 1986; Ogle, 1992)

The K–W–L is a three step teaching/learning framework designed to guide and to motivate students as they read to acquire information from expository text. The strategy helps students to think about what they know or believe they know about a topic; what they need to find out by reading the text; and finally what they learned by reading and what they still need/want to learn about the topic from other information sources. The first two steps in the model are pre-reading activities. The beginning step, **K–What I KNOW**, involves brainstorming with students to help them focus on their prior knowledge, then categorizing what they know. The next step, **W–WHAT do I want to learn**, uses the results of the brainstorming and categorizing by having students identify areas of controversy and/or key categories that contain little or no information to develop a purpose for reading. In the final step, **L–what I LEARNED**, students record their findings as they read, or immediately after reading, to assess whether their questions/concerns were resolved. The K–W–L model is outlined on a worksheet that students can use as they proceed through the steps of the strategy (see the example on p. 140).

Procedure:

- Present the concept to be studied and engage students in oral discussion/ brainstorming. The teacher's questions should lead students to think about and to respond *specifically* to the topic being discussed.

- The student's responses are recorded on the chalkboard or on an overhead. The teacher, however, does not merely accept student's ideas/statements. The teacher should encourage students to extend their thinking by asking questions that require them to consider the source and substance of their information. Ask students where they learned their information and how they could "prove" that what they said is correct.
- Facilitate organizing students' statements into general categories of information that they may come across as they read and discuss the kinds of information that they are likely to find in the text.
- Help students identify areas of controversy and/or key categories that contain little or no information to develop a purpose for reading. Complete this step as a group activity, but have students write the questions that they are most interested in learning about on their worksheets so that personal interest will guide and motivate their reading.
- During or immediately after reading, have students record their findings on their sheets.
- During class discussion, record what was learned on the board and help students assess whether their questions/concerns were answered by reading the text.
- Guide students to other sources of information for questions or concerns that were not satisfactorily addressed by the text.

K-What we KNOW	W-What we WANT to find out or need to learn	L-What we LEARNED and still want to learn

Categories of information we expect to use:

A.   B.

C.   D.

E.   F.

Options:

- Students who are young or not accustomed to the categorization process in the first step of K–W–L may need additional support and practice. To begin, the teacher can think aloud in order to demonstrate how key categories are determined then invite students to offer additional categories.

• The use of K–W–L should be adapted to the complexity and length of the text. Decide whether students can read and gain information by reading the whole text, or if it should be broken into logical chunks that provide opportunities for students to think about what they are reading.

LINK (LIST, INQUIRE, NOTE, KNOW) (Based on Vaughan and Estes, 1986)

LINK is a pre-reading strategy similar to brainstorming, designed to help students make links between their prior knowledge and the content they will be studying. This strategy incorporates writing, shared brainstorming, and discussion. The opportunity for discussion, reflection, and clarification allows students to explore various associations. Students are more aware of the topic, establish links to their prior knowledge, are able to think of more information when they move to the final step, and are motivated to study more carefully. The strategy is ideal when you suspect that there is minimal background knowledge on the topic among your students.

If you are using this strategy with Chapter 2, use the key term "Social Studies" or the topic "Teaching Social Studies."

Procedure:

• The teacher writes the topic or key term on the board or overhead transparency. The term should be familiar enough so that it will trigger responses among all students. Give students three minutes to **list** all associations they make with the key term. The purpose of this step is to have students make as many connections from their prior knowledge to the topic as possible.

• Call on all students one at a time to share a unique response. The teacher or a scribe writes these responses on the board or overhead transparency. Allow students to offer more ideas if time permits. The purpose of this step is to maximize student participation.

• After all responses are given, the teacher should invite the class to **inquire** about individual students' associations. The teacher facilitates but does not answer questions, because the students are the ones who are clarifying their connections and elaborating on their understandings. The teacher records student questions for future reference. The purpose of this step is to have students share, clarify, and elaborate their understandings so that they discover errors, engage in controversy, and identify questions while bringing prior awareness to the surface.

• After the inquiring is complete and all questions have been recorded, erase the responses or turn off the overhead projector. Tell students to **note** everything that they **know** in one minute in response to the same cue. At the end of one minute, have the students reflect on the differences between their initial list and their new list. The purpose of this step is to identify connections they didn't initially make, validate what they do know, and set purposes for reading.

POST-GRAPHIC ORGANIZER (Based on Richardson and Morgan, 2003)

A before-, during-, and after-reading strategy that facilitates collaboration and helps students become familiar with the structure of knowledge in specific content areas. The underlying processes include prediction about textual content and the structure of knowledge of that content, summarizing information, and organizing information in a way that represents the structure of the knowledge. Although this strategy works well in all content areas, it is particularly effective for understanding scientific and mathematical processes.

Procedure:

- Students preview the selection to determine the topic, structure, and main ideas.
- Students work in small groups to hypothesize the best form for the graphic organizer.
- Students read the selection silently to gather information for the group's graphic organizer.
- The group meets to discuss and create the post-graphic organizer based on the information each member has gathered. Each group prepares a large model that will be shared with the class.
- Each group presents their model to the class.
- After all models have been presented, have students reflect on how they might change their model to better depict the structure of what they learned.

Options:

- For younger students or students not used to creating graphic organizers, consider sharing graphic organizers designed to reflect expository text structure. Then create a post-graphic organizer with the whole class using a combination of think-aloud and student input to model the construction process. You may have to repeat this process several times, gradually releasing responsibility for the construction to students in order to scaffold them into independent group work.
- Consider using "Categorization" prior to using Post Graphic Organizers to scaffold students into the process.

PREDICTION (Based on Smith, 1988; Vacca and Vacca, 2002)

A before-reading strategy that helps students activate prior knowledge about concepts before reading. To predict, students rely on what they know to make educated guesses about the concept or text to be read. Predicting is an underlying process in strategies such as Anticipation Guides and Directed Reading–Thinking Activity (DR-TA). Since predicting is a flexible strategy that requires minimal teacher preparation, it is particularly useful when planning time or class time for a pre-reading strategy is limited.

If you are using this strategy with Chapter 3, preview the title, headings, subheadings, and illustrations (pictures, figures, etc.) to predict what the chapter will be about.

PreP (PRE READING PLAN) (Based on Langer, 1981; Vacca and Vacca, 2002)

A before-reading strategy that helps students activate prior knowledge and provides the teacher with practical information about how students' concepts and language correspond with the text. Brainstorming associations, reflecting, and elaborating are underlying processes in this strategy. PreP is especially helpful for teachers when trying to assess students' background knowledge and figuring out how to facilitate comprehension. Typically, the following three levels can be identified:

- Much background—students are able to define the concept, draw analogies, think categorically, and make conceptual links.
- Some background—students can cite characteristics and give examples, but are unable to make connections or articulate relationships between their prior knowledge and the new material.
- Little background—students can only give words that sound like the concept word or make simple associations that are not conceptually linked to the topic.

If you are using this strategy with Chapter 3, use the key term "Interdisciplinary Instruction."

Procedure:

- Prior to class, the teacher examines the text to identify pictures, phrases, and keywords that represent the major concepts.
- During phase one, provide students the opportunity to identify any associations they have from their prior knowledge with the key concept by saying, "Tell us something that comes to mind when you hear the word [keyword identified from text]."
- List student responses on the board.
- During phase two, encourage students to reflect on their initial responses to develop awareness of their associations by probing their memories. Have them elaborate on their initial responses by saying, "Why did you think of [student response]?" By listening to each other's explanations, students can critically evaluate, revise, and integrate associations into their own pool of knowledge.
- During phase three, push students to reformulate their knowledge by verbalizing associations that have been changed or elaborated through discussion. Initiate this discussion by saying, "Before we read the text, do you have any new ideas based on our discussion?"

Options:

- Consider using a concrete object in place of a keyword when working with less sophisticated students. For example, when introducing the concept of economics or entrepreneurship hold up a dollar bill and say, "Tell us something that comes to mind when you see this."

Teaching and Learning Strategies
Referenced in Chapters

PROGRESSIVE CINQUAIN (Based on Vaughan and Estes, 1986)

An after-reading strategy that helps students synthesize their learning while sharing, perception-checking their understanding, and collaborating on increasingly sophisticated written summaries utilizing a cinquain poetry format. The underlying processes include summarizing and synthesizing content while small groups provide a more extensive basis for new associations and the opportunity for pooling ideas. This strategy works well with both narrative and expository text.

Procedure:

- Provide the model of a cinquain poem shown below.
- Assign a topic (not a title) based on the reading or learning that was just completed.
- Each student writes a cinquain independently.
- As individual students finish, pair them up to share their poems and collaboratively write a new cinquain that is a combination of what they have written or a new one that is better.
- As pairs of students complete their new cinquain, combine two pairs of students into a foursome and have them share and collaboratively write a new cinquain that is either a combination of what the two pairs have written or something entirely new.
- Have students write their final product on chart paper or the board.
- Each group shares their progressive cinquain with the entire class.
- Engage the students in discussion about which cinquain reflects an in depth understanding of the topic and why.

Options:

- For younger students or those that have not had experience writing cinquains, complete the cinquain as a whole class or brainstorm lists of words for each line of the poem before having students write.
- For older students, consider having the class vote for which cinquain best reflects an understanding of the topic.
- Try other poetry formats such as biopoems.

Cinquain Format

Title (one word)	———
Description (two adjectives)	——— ———
Action (three "ing" words)	——— ——— ———
Feeling (four word phrase)	——— ——— ——— ———
Synonym for title (one word)	———

PROGRESSIVE WRITING

An after-reading strategy that helps students collaboratively create a written record of what they were thinking and learning. Progressive writing encourages all individuals to participate, shift point of view, make logical connections, summarize, and engage in critical thinking. This strategy is particularly good when individuals are reluctant writers or are hesitant to share their individual writing with the class.

Procedure:

- Have students form equal small groups of 3 to 4 students each.
- Provide a writing prompt such as: "What did you learn from your reading?" or "What did you think about. . . ?"
- Have each student begin writing their response on a sheet of paper.
- After 5 minutes, call time and ask students to pass their paper to the next person in their group. The next person reads what was written and then picks up the writing where the previous writer left off. After 5 minutes, call time and ask students to pass their papers again. Repeat the above process until the paper comes back to the student who started the writing.
- When the paper, has returned to the student who started it, he or she should read the entire document and write a conclusion. Give the students 5 to 10 minutes to write.
- Have each student read aloud the collaboratively written paper he or she is holding, or have the students pass around the papers until each group member has had a chance to read each paper.
- Have each group decide which paper to share with the entire class and select a reader to present.

Options:

- Have the class vote on which paper they believe best expresses the ideas presented in the text. Post it on a bulletin board or make copies for each student.

SAVE THE LAST WORD FOR ME (Based on Work Originally Developed by Carolyn Burke and Described in Newman, 1983)

A during- and after-reading strategy designed to enhance text understanding, foster group interaction/problem-solving, provide a "scaffold" for challenging text material, and encourage purposeful note-taking.

Procedure:

- Students form groups of three.
- Students read the text (or portions of the text) silently.

- On the index cards or half sheets of paper, they note areas of agreement/ disagreement with the author and/or questions that occur to them while reading.
- Students discuss the text (or portions of the text). Each member of the group selects a comment or question from the note cards for the group to discuss. Other members of the group react to the comment or question by sharing their own opinions, in the case of areas of agreement/disagreement, or by attempting answers, in the case of questions.
- The student who initially shared the comment/question has the "last word" by summarizing the discussion and offering his/her own opinion.
- Another member of the group shares a comment/question, and the discussion cycle begins again.

Options:

Consider having students use INSERT during reading to help students identify the three most important points in the text. Then have students write a "pithy quote" illustrating each important point noting the page number on the front of an index card and a reason why the student thought it was important on the back of the card. The reason can be shared as the "last word". After the entire text has been read/discussed, the group can summarize important issues/questions. A recorder can take notes of this summary discussion for sharing with the entire class.

SEMANTIC MAPPING (Based on Heimlich and Pittelman, 1986) and GRAPHIC ORGANIZERS FOR EXPOSITORY TEXT STRUCTURE

A before-, during-, or after-reading strategy that helps students graphically organize or categorize information. These organizing and categorizing processes are the basis of many strategies such as Graphic Organizers and List-Group-Label. Organizing and classifying information helps students become more active readers while they learn how to cognitively organize vocabulary/technical terms to gain insight and understanding of larger concepts. The following procedure will focus on semantic mapping as a before-, during-, and after-reading strategy.

If you are using this strategy with chapter 2 use the core concept "Teaching World History." (See Exhibit **6.)**

Procedure:

- Prior to reading, give students a concept or core question that will be the main focus of the map.
- Discuss the focus and have students generate questions that can help explain the concept or question.

- Have students read individually or in pairs to answer the questions that they generated and find other information that explains the concept or answers the core question.
- After reading, have the students form small groups and list everything they remember about the concept on index cards.
- Write the concept in the center of the chalkboard and circle it. Ask students for the main categories of information that they found while reading to create the strands (see Exhibit 6).
- Continue modeling the process with strands and details until the students are ready to create their own semantic map in their small groups with their index cards.
- After groups have come to some agreement on the arrangement of their index cards, have the groups share and discuss their maps with the whole class.
- Finally, have students create their own semantic map on a piece of paper for their own notes.

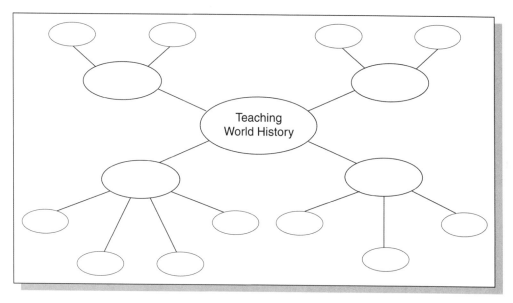

Teaching
World History

EXHIBIT 6

Options:

- For younger students or those less familiar with the semantic mapping process, facilitate the construction of the semantic map on the board by having groups attach their cards to the board and use them to create a whole class map.
- For older students and those familiar with the semantic mapping process, allow students to define their own core concept and generate their own map in small groups or individually.

Descriptive Text Structure

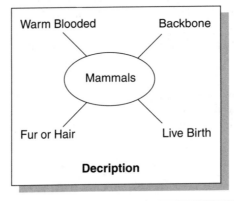

Decription

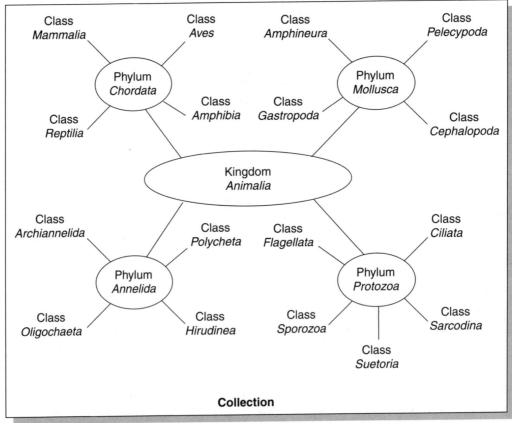

Collection

Sequential Text Structure

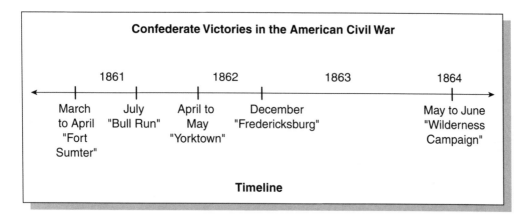

Confederate Victories in the American Civil War

1861   1862   1863   1864

March   July   April to   December   May to June
to April   "Bull Run"   May   "Fredericksburg"   "Wilderness
"Fort   "Yorktown"   Campaign"
Sumter"

Timeline

Steps in Changing a Light Bulb
1. Purchase new light bulb
2. Turn off light switch
3. Unscrew old light bulb
4. Screw in new light bulb
5. Turn on light switch
6. Dispose of burned out light bulb

Procedure

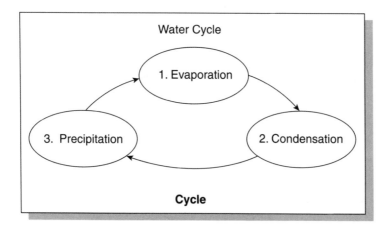

Water Cycle

1. Evaporation

3. Precipitation

2. Condensation

Cycle

Compare/Contrast Text Structure

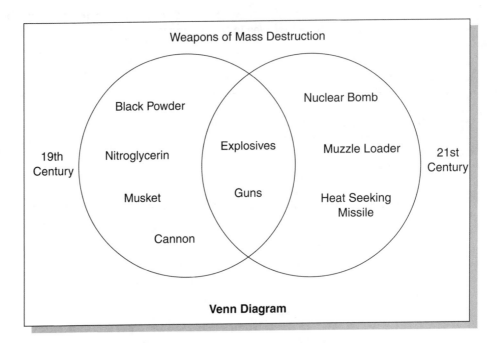

Venn Diagram

Periods / Life and Time	Cretaceous	Jurassic	Triassic
Aquatic Life	Modern Bony Fishes	Plesiosaurs and Icthyosaurs	Ammonites
Terrestrial LIfe	Snakes, Lizards	Dinosaurs	Crocodiles
Time that Period Began	135,000,000 Years Ago	180,000,000 Years Ago	230,000,000 Years Ago

Mesozoic Era

Attributes Chart

Cause/Effect Text Structure

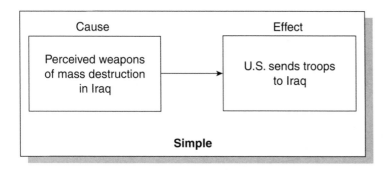

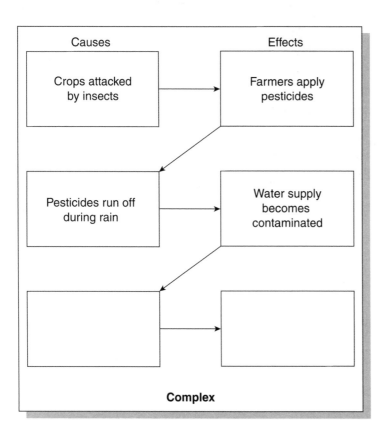

Problem/Solution Text Structure

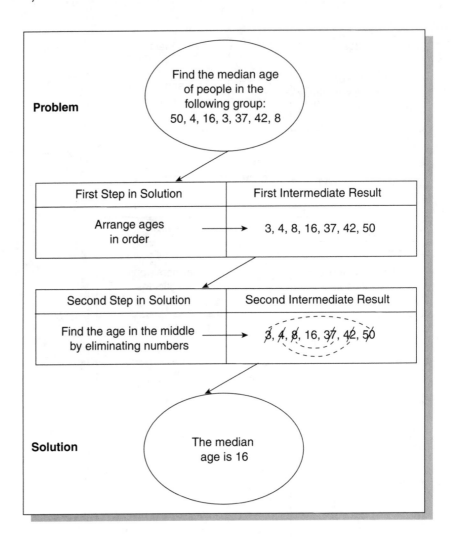

SKETCH TO STRETCH (Based on Harste, Burke, Siegel, and Feathers in Tierney, Readence, and Dishner, 1990)

An after-reading strategy that helps students represent the most important "picture" that plays in their mind when they read a selection. It also gives students the opportunity to see that varied meanings are constructed by different class members as they share and discuss their drawings. This strategy provides students with an opportunity to discuss the impact the text had upon them by deciding upon and then sharing the most important mental image that was formed as they interacted with the text. During this sharing, the concept is reinforced that reading text is much more than just "saying the words." Mental images must be formed. The strategy is useful for both content and narrative text.

Procedure:

- Students read the text.
- Instruct students to draw a sketch of the picture they see in their minds when they think about the information presented or the story. Remind students that there is not a "right" or "wrong" picture because there are many ways of depicting meaning.
- If all students have been reading the same text, they should divide into groups of four or five after completing their sketches. Each person shows his or her sketch to the others in the group. Group members have a chance to express what they think the artist/student is trying to say.
- After all the group members have had the opportunity to indicate what they think the drawing represents, the artist/student gets the last word.
- Each group shares with the whole group by collaborating and constructing a group sketch after sharing, choosing one sketch from the group to share, or sharing all of the sketches if time permits.
- Sketches may be put on an overhead projector or displayed on poster board.

Options:

- This strategy may also be implemented with text that the teacher reads aloud to the class or a small group of students.

SUMMARIZATION (Based on Vacca and Vacca, 2002)

An after-reading strategy that helps students reduce a text to its main points. To become good at summarizing, students must be sensitive to text structure and the way the author organizes ideas, and be able to identify important ideas. Identifying important information and putting this information in their own words are the underlying processes in strategies such as GRASP, Paired Summarizing, and Progressive Cinquain.

Procedure:

Have students write a rough draft following these guidelines:

- Include only important points and delete unnecessary detail.
- Collapse lists by using a term that describes the broad category or concept.
- Use topic sentences from the text or create your own when there aren't any.
- Integrate the information into a coherent piece of writing.

Have students polish and rewrite the summary in their own words to get a solid grasp on the main points.

Options:

Students may have difficulty generating polished summaries at first. Consider writing a polished summary yourself and have students compare their summaries with your version, or have students share their summaries in small groups. Another option is to present the class with three summaries (one that is good, one that is fair, and one that is poor) and have them compare and contrast. Regardless of the comparison process used, have students reflect on how they might improve their writing next time.

THINK-PAIR-SHARE (Adapted from Judy Richardson and Raymond Morgan, 2003)

A before-, during-, or after-reading strategy designed to maximize student participation and foster student interaction when time is limited. This strategy can also be used to enhance understanding of text, provide a "scaffold" for challenging text material, and foster interaction/problem-solving.

Procedure:

- Students form groups of *two.*
- The teacher provides a prompt before or after reading.
- Students individually brainstorm their ideas on half-sheets of paper.
- Students share their ideas with their partner.
- The teacher circulates to listen to partner discussions and targets one or two sets of partners to share with the entire group.

Option for During Reading:

- Students form groups of *two.*
- Students read a portion of the text silently (usually one or two paragraphs).
- When both have finished reading, one student serves as a listener.
- Reteller explains what was read while listener interrupts only for clarification.
- When reteller is finished, the listener points out ideas summarized incorrectly and adds ideas left out. The pair then works together to clarify and elaborate upon their understanding.
- Change roles and begin on the next portion of the text.

YOUR OWN QUESTIONS (Based on Vacca and Vacca, 2002)

A before-, during-, and after-reading strategy that helps students engage in active comprehension. Student-generated questions stimulate interest and draw learners into the text because students will read to resolve their own conceptual conflicts while satisfying their own purposes. The process of students generating their own questions forms the basis for strategies such as ReQuest and Expectation Outlines.

Procedure:

- Have students preview the material by looking at the major headings, subheading, figures, and tables in the text.
- Ask students to write several questions that they think will be answered when they read the text.
- Discuss several of the student-generated questions and list them on the board.
- Have students read the text and find out which questions are answered.
- After reading, have students discuss which questions were answered, which questions were not answered, why some questions were not answered, and where students might look to find answers to their questions that were not addressed in the text.

Options:

The teacher can read aloud a few paragraphs from the beginning of the text or students can read these paragraphs silently rather than previewing the whole selection. This works particularly well with narrative text.

REFERENCES FOR TEACHING AND LEARNING STRATEGIES

Alvermann, D. E. (1991). The discussion web: A graphic aid for learning across the curriculum. *The Reading Teacher, 45*, 92–99.

Alvermann, D. E., & Moore, D. W. (1991). Secondary school reading. In R. Barr, M. L. Kamil, P. B. Mosenthal, & P. D. Pearson (Eds.), *Handbook of reading research: Volume 2*, 951–983. New York: Longman.

Bean, T. W. (2000). Reading in the content areas: Social constructivist dimensions. In M. L. Kamil, P. B. Mosenthal, P. D. Pearson, and R. Barr. (Eds.) *Handbook of reading research: Volume 3*, 629–644. Mahwah, NJ: Erlbaum.

Burke, C. as described in Newman, J. (1983), *Whole language activities*. Halifax, NS: Department of Education, Dalhousie University.

Brozo, W. G. & Simpson, M. L. (2003). *Readers, teachers, learners: Expanding literacy across the content areas, 4th ed.* Upper Saddle River, NJ: Merrill/Prentice Hall.

Carr, E., & Ogle, D. (1987). K–W–L plus: A strategy for comprehension and summarization. *Journal of Reading, 30*, 626–631.

Caulkins, L. M. (1986). *The art of teaching writing.* Portsmouth, NH: Heinemann.

Jerry Harste, Carolyn Burke, Mjorie Siegel, and Karen Feathers (Tierney, Readence, & Dishner, 1990)

Langer, J. A. (1981). From theory to practice: A prereading plan. *Journal of Reading, 25,* 152–156.

Manzo, A. V., & Manzo, U. C. (1990). *Content area reading: A heuristic approach.* Columbus, OH: Merrill.

Nist, S. L., & Simpson, M. L. (2000). College Studying. In M. L. Kamil, P. B. Mosenthal, P. D. Pearson, and R. Barr (Eds.), *Handbook of reading research: Volume 3,* 645–666. Mahwah, NJ: Erlbaum.

Ogle, D. M. (1986). K–W–L: A teaching model that develops active reading of expository text. *The Reading Teacher, 39,* 564–570.

Ogle, D. M. (1992). K–W–L in action: Secondary teachers find applications that work. In E. K. Dishner, T. W. Bean, J. E. Readence, and D. W. Moore (Eds.), *Reading in the content areas: Improving classroom instruction, 3rd ed.,* 270–282. Dubuque, IA: Kendall/Hunt.

Paris, S. C., Wasik, B. A., & Turner, G. C. (1991). The development of strategic reading. In R. Barr, M. L. Kamil, P. B. Mosenthal, & P. D. Pearson (Eds.), *Handbook of reading research: Volume 2,* 609–640. New York: Longman.

Richardson, J. S., & Morgan, R. F. (2003). *Reading to learn in the content areas, 5th ed.* Belmont, CA: Wadsworth.

Schwartz, R. (1988). Learning to learn: Vocabulary in content area textbooks. *Journal of Reading, 32*(2), 108–118.

Schwartz, R. M., & Raphael, T. E. (1985). Concept of definition: A key to improving students' vocabulary. *Reading Teacher, 39,* 198–204.

Short, K. G., Harste, J. C., & Burke, C. (1996). *Creating classrooms for authors and inquirers, 2nd ed.* Portsmouth, NH: Heinemann.

Stauffer, R. (1969). *Directing reading maturity as a cognitive process.* New York: Harper & Row.

Tierney, R. J., Readence, J. E., & Dishner, E. K. (1995). *Reading strategies and practices: A compendium, 4th ed.* Boston: Allyn & Bacon.

Vacca, R. T., & Vacca, J. L. (2002). *Content area reading: Literacy and learning across the curriculum.* Boston: Allyn & Bacon.

Vaughan, J. L., & Estes, T. H. (1986). *Reading and reasoning beyond the primary grades.* Boston: Allyn & Bacon.

Wade, S. E., & Moje, E. B. (2000). The role of text in classroom learning. M. L. Kamil, P. B. Mosenthal, P. D. Pearson, and R. Barr (Eds.), In *Handbook of reading research: Volume 3,* 609–643. Mahwah, NJ: Erlbaum.

National Standards and Goals

THE NATIONAL STRATEGIC PLAN AND ACTION AGENDA FOR AGRICULTURAL EDUCATION

www.teamaged.org/plan2020/plan_cover.htm

Goal 1: An abundance of highly motivated, well-educated teachers in all disciplines, pre-kindergarten through adult, providing agriculture, food, fiber, and natural resources systems education.

- Agricultural education leaders ensure a sufficient quantity of qualified agriculture teachers who represent the demographics of the nation.
- Preparation programs for all elementary, secondary, and adult teachers integrate instruction in agriculture, food, fiber, and natural resources systems.
- Agricultural education leaders provide relevant instructional leadership and professional development opportunities for themselves and all teachers.
- Teacher preparation programs rely on the most current and broadly representative research for developing curriculum and courses of study.
- Partnerships of leaders in agriculture, food, fiber, and natural resources systems education, industry and government provide diverse learning experiences to ensure that school administrators and counselors are aware of the broad career opportunities available in agriculture.
- Agricultural education leaders provide instruction in the review, selection, adaptation, and use of appropriate educational technologies and teaching strategies to address the changing education environment.

Goal 2: All students have access to seamless, lifelong instruction in agriculture, food, fiber, and natural resources systems through a wide variety of delivery methods and educational settings.

- Collaboration among educators and educational entities ensure students benefit from educational effectiveness and efficiency.
- All students in urban, suburban, and rural schools have access to high-quality agricultural education programs.
- Students are prepared for successful careers in global agriculture, food, fiber, and natural resources systems.

- Every agriculture student has opportunities for experiential learning and leadership development.
- Agricultural education instructional systems and materials provide for diverse learning styles.
- Student enrollments in agricultural education represent the diversity of the school-aged population.

Goal 3: All students are conversationally literate in agriculture, food, fiber, and natural resources systems.

- Agriculture teachers encourage cross-curricular course development and instructional collaboration with teachers in all disciplines.
- All teachers include elements of agriculture in a relevant, integrated instructional approach.
- Agriculture teachers collaborate with other groups to bring factual information about agriculture, food, fiber and natural resources systems to all students.

Goal 4: Partnerships and strategic alliances ensure a continuous presence of education in and about agriculture, food, fiber, and natural resources.

- Positive working relationships with multiple stakeholders build lines of communication and provide a diverse work force for the agriculture, food, fiber, and natural resources industries.
- Broad-based coalitions of groups and organizations collaborate to develop and disseminate contemporary agriculture curricula for all students.
- Partnerships and strategic alliances provide strong support for agricultural education.
- Numerous and varied stakeholders, inside and outside of the school system, engage in a continuing effort to strengthen and refine the shared vision, mission and goals.

IRA/NCTE STANDARDS FOR THE ENGLISH LANGUAGE ARTS

www.ncte.org/standards/standards.shtml

The vision guiding these standards is that all students must have the opportunities and resources to develop the language skills they need to pursue life's goals and to participate fully as informed, productive members of society. These standards assume that literacy growth begins before children enter school as they experience and experiment with literacy activities—reading and writing, and associating spoken words with their graphic representations. Recognizing this fact, these standards encourage the development of curriculum and instruction that make productive use of the emerging literacy abilities that children bring to school. Furthermore, the standards provide ample room for the innovation and creativity essential to teaching and learning. They are not prescriptions for particular curriculum or instruction.

Although we present these standards as a list, we want to emphasize that they are not distinct and separable; they are, in fact, interrelated and should be considered as a whole:

- Students read a wide range of print and nonprint texts to build an understanding of texts, of themselves, and of the cultures of the United States and the world; to acquire new information; to respond to the needs and demands of society and the workplace; and for personal fulfillment. Among these texts are fiction and nonfiction, classic and contemporary works.
- Students read a wide range of literature from many periods in many genres to build an understanding of the many dimensions (e.g., philosophical, ethical, aesthetic) of human experience.
- Students apply a wide range of strategies to comprehend, interpret, evaluate, and appreciate texts. They draw on their prior experience, their interactions with other readers and writers, their knowledge of word meaning and of other texts, their word identification strategies, and their understanding of textual features (e.g., sound–letter correspondence, sentence structure, context, graphics).
- Students adjust their own use of spoken, written, and visual language (e.g., conventions, style, vocabulary) to communicate effectively with a variety of audiences for a variety of purposes.
- Students employ a wide range of strategies as they write and use different writing process elements appropriately to communicate with different audiences for a variety of purposes.
- Students apply knowledge of language structure, language conventions (e.g., spelling and punctuation), media techniques, figurative language, and genre to create, critique, and discuss print and nonprint texts.
- Students conduct research on issues and interests by generating ideas and questions, and by posing problems. They gather, evaluate, and synthesize data from a variety of sources (e.g., print and nonprint texts, artifacts, people) to communicate their discoveries in ways that suit their purpose and audience.
- Students use a variety of technological and informational resources (e.g., libraries, databases, computer networks, video) to gather and synthesize information and to create and communicate knowledge.
- Students develop an understanding of and respect for diversity in language use, patterns, and dialects across cultures, ethnic groups, geographic regions, and social roles.
- Students whose first language is not English make use of their first language to develop competency in the English language arts and to develop understanding of content across the curriculum.
- Students participate as knowledgeable, reflective, creative, and critical members of a variety of literacy communities.
- Students use spoken, written, and visual language to accomplish their own purpose (e.g., for learning, enjoyment, persuasion, and the exchange for information).

National Standards and Goals

TEACHERS OF ENGLISH TO SPEAKERS OF OTHER LANGUAGES

ESL Standards for Pre-k–12 Students

http://www.tesol.org/assoc/k12standards/it/01.html

NATIONAL COUNCIL OF TEACHERS OF MATHEMATICS STANDARDS

http://nctm.org/standards/standards.htm

Number and Operations Standard for Grades 6–12

- Understand patterns, relations, and functions by being able to represent, analyze, and generalize a variety of patterns with tables, graphs, words, and, when possible, symbolic rules (grades 6–8).
- Represent and analyze mathematical situations and structures using algebraic symbols by being able to represent, analyze, and generalize a variety of patterns with tables, graphs, words, and, when possible, symbolic rules (6–8).
- Use mathematical models to represent and understand quantitative relationships: represent and understand quantitative relationships: model and solve contextualized problems using various representations, such as graphs, tables, and equations (6–8).
- Understand numbers, ways of representing numbers, relationships among numbers, and number systems by being able to develop a deeper understanding of very large and very small numbers and of various representations of them (9–12).
- Understand meanings of operations and how they relate to one another by being able to judge the effects of such operations as multiplication, division, and computing powers and roots on the magnitudes of quantities (9–12).
- Compute fluently and make reasonable estimates to be able to develop fluency in operations with real numbers, vectors, and matrices, using mental computation or paper-and-pencil calculations for simple cases and technology for more-complicated cases (9–12).

Algebra Standard for Grades 6–12

- Understand meanings of operations and how they relate to one another by being able to understand the meaning and effects of arithmetic operations with fractions, decimals, and integers (6–8).
- Compute fluently and make reasonable estimates by being able to select appropriate methods and tools for computing with fractions and decimals from among mental computation, estimation, calculators or computers, and paper and pencil, depending on the situation, and apply the selected methods (grades 6–8).

- Understand patterns, relations, and functions by being able to work flexibly with fractions, decimals, and percents to solve problems (6–8) and by generalizing patterns using explicitly defined and recursively defined functions(9–12).
- Represent and analyze mathematical situations and structures using algebraic symbols by being able to understand the meaning of equivalent forms of expressions, equations, inequalities, and relations (9–12).
- Use mathematical models to represent and understand quantitative relationships by being able to identify essential quantitative relationships in a situation and determine the class or classes of functions that might model the relationships (9–12).
- Analyze change in various contexts by being able to approximate and interpret rates of change from graphical and numerical data (9–12).

Geometry Standard for Grades 6-12

- Analyze characteristics and properties of two- and three-dimensional geometric shapes and develop mathematical arguments about geometric relationships by being able to precisely describe, classify, and understand relationships among types of two- and three-dimensional objects using their defining properties (6–8) and by being able to analyze properties and determine attributes of two- and three-dimensional objects (9–12).
- Specify locations and describe spatial relationships using coordinate geometry and other representational systems by being able to use coordinate geometry to represent and examine the properties of geometric shapes (6–8) and by being able to use Cartesian coordinates and other coordinate systems, such as navigational, polar, or spherical systems, to analyze geometric situations; investigate conjectures and solve problems involving two- and three-dimensional objects represented with Cartesian coordinates (9–12).
- Apply transformations and use symmetry to analyze mathematical situations by being able to describe sizes, positions, and orientations of shapes under informal transformations such as flips, turns, slides, and scaling (6–8) and by being able to understand and represent translations, reflections, rotations, and dilations of objects in the plane by using sketches, coordinates, vectors, function notation, and matrices (9–12).
- Use visualization, spatial reasoning, and geometric modeling to solve problems by being able to draw geometric objects with specified properties, such as side lengths or angle measures (6–8) and by being able to draw and construct representations of two- and three-dimensional geometric objects using a variety of tools (9–12).

Measurement Standard for Grades 6-12

- Understand measurable attributes of objects and the units, systems, and processes of measurement by being able to understand both metric and customary systems of measurement (6–8) and by being able to make decisions about units and scales that are appropriate for problem situations involving measurement (9–12).
- Apply appropriate techniques, tools, and formulas to determine measurements by being able to use common benchmarks to select appropriate methods for esti-

mating measurements (6–8) and by being able to analyze precision, accuracy, and approximate error in measurement situations (9–12).

Data Analysis and Probability Standard for Grades 6-12

- Formulate questions that can be addressed with data and collect, organize, and display relevant data to answer them and be able to formulate questions, design studies, and collect data about a characteristic shared by two populations or different characteristics within one population (6–8) and be able to understand the differences among various kinds of studies and which types of inferences can legitimately be drawn from each; know the characteristics of well-designed studies, including the role of randomization in surveys and experiments (9–12).
- Select and use appropriate statistical methods to analyze data by being able to find, use, and interpret measures of center and spread, including mean and interquartile range (6–8) and be able to (for univariate measurement data) display the distribution, describe its shape, and select and calculate summary statistics (9–12).
- Develop and evaluate inferences and predictions that are based on data by being able to use observations about differences between two or more samples to make conjectures about the populations from which the samples were taken (6–12) and by being able to use simulations to explore the variability of sample statistics from a known population and to construct sampling distributions (9–12).
- Understand and apply basic concepts of probability by being able to understand and use appropriate terminology to describe complementary and mutually exclusive events (6–8) and by being able to understand the concepts of sample space and probability distribution and construct sample spaces and distributions in simple cases (9–12).

Problem Solving Standard for Grades 6-12

- Students should be able to solve problems that arise in mathematics and in other contexts.

Reasoning and Proof Standard for Grades 6-12

- Students should be able to recognize reasoning and proof as fundamental aspects of mathematics.

Communication Standard for Grades 6-12

- Students should be able to organize and consolidate their mathematical thinking through communication.

Connections Standard for Grades 6-12

- Students should be able to recognize and use connections among mathematical ideas.

Representation Standard for Grades 6–12

- Students should be able to create and use representations to organize, record, and communicate mathematical ideas.

NATIONAL SCIENCE EDUCATION STANDARDS

www.nap.edu/readingroom/books/nses/html/overview.html#teaching

Teaching Standard A: Teachers of science plan an inquiry-based science program for their students. In doing this, teachers

- Develop a framework of yearlong and short-term goals for students.
- Select science content and adapt and design curricula to meet the interests, knowledge, understanding, abilities, and experience of students.
- Select teaching and assessment strategies that support the development of student understanding and nurture a community of science learners.
- Work together as colleagues within and across disciplines and grade levels.

Teaching Standard B: Teachers of science guide and facilitate learning. In doing this, teachers

- Focus and support inquiries while interacting with students.
- Orchestrate discourse among students about scientific ideas.
- Challenge students to accept and share responsibility for their own learning.
- Recognize and respond to student diversity and encourage all students to participate fully in science learning.
- Encourage and model the skills of scientific inquiry, as well as the curiosity, openness to new ideas and data and skepticism that characterize science.

Teaching Standard C: Teachers of science engage in ongoing assessment of their teaching and of student learning. In doing this, teachers

- Use multiple methods and systematically gather data about student understanding and ability.
- Analyze assessment data to guide teaching.
- Guide students in self-assessment.
- Use student data, observations of teaching, and interactions with colleagues to reflect on and improve teaching practice.
- Use student data, observations of teaching, and interactions with colleagues to report student achievement and opportunities to learn to students, teachers, parents, policy makers, and the general public.

Teaching Standard D: Teachers of science design and manage learning environments that provide students with the time, space, and resources needed for learning science. In doing this, teachers

- Structure the time available so that students are able to engage in extended investigations.

- Create a setting for student work that is flexible and supportive of science inquiry.
- Ensure a safe working environment.
- Make the available science tools, materials, media, and technological resources accessible to students.
- Identify and use resources outside the school.
- Engage students in designing the learning environment.

Teaching Standard E: Teachers of science develop communities of science learners that reflect the intellectual rigor of scientific inquiry and the attitudes and social values conducive to scientific learning. In doing this, teachers

- Display and demand respect for the diverse ideas, skills, and experiences of all students.
- Enable students to have significant voice in decisions about the content and context of their work and require students to take responsibility for the learning of all members of the community.
- Nurture collaboration among students.
- Structure and facilitate ongoing formal and informal discussion based on a shared understanding of rules of scientific discourse.
- Model and emphasize the skills, attitudes, and values of scientific inquiry.

Teaching Standard F: Teachers of science actively participate in the ongoing planning and development of the school science program. In doing this, teachers

- Plan and develop the school science program.
- Participate in decisions concerning the allocation of time and other resources to the science program.
- Participate fully in planning and implementing professional growth and development strategies for themselves and their colleagues.

NATIONAL COUNCIL FOR THE SOCIAL STUDIES: NATIONAL STANDARDS FOR SOCIAL STUDIES TEACHERS

http://peabody.vanderbilt.edu/depts/tandl/faculty/myers/standards.html

Culture and Cultural Diversity: Social studies teachers should possess the knowledge, capabilities, and dispositions to organize and provide instruction at the appropriate school level for the study of Culture and Cultural Diversity.

Time, Continuity, and Change: Social studies teachers should possess the knowledge, capabilities, and dispositions to organize and provide instruction at the appropriate school level for the study of Time, Continuity, and Change.

People, Places, and Environment: Social studies teachers should possess the knowledge, capabilities, and dispositions to organize and provide instructions at the appropriate school level for the study of People, Places, and Environments.

Individual Development and Identity: Social studies teachers should possess the knowledge, capabilities, and dispositions to organize and provide instruction at the appropriate school level for the study of Individual Development and Identity.

Individuals, Groups, and Institutions: Social studies teachers should possess the knowledge, capabilities, and dispositions to organize and provide instruction at the appropriate school level for the study of interactions among Individuals, Groups, and Institutions.

Power, Authority, and Governance: Social studies teachers should possess the knowledge, capabilities, and dispositions to organize and provide instruction at the appropriate school level for the study of Power, Authority, and Governance.

Production, Distribution, and Consumption: Social studies teachers should possess the knowledge, capabilities, and dispositions to organize and provide instruction at the appropriate school level for the study of how people organize for the Production, Distribution, and Consumption of Goods and Services.

Science, Technology, and Society: Social studies teachers should possess the knowledge, capabilities, and dispositions to organize and provide instruction at the appropriate school level for the study of Science, Technology, and Society.

Global Connections: Social studies teachers should possess the knowledge, capabilities, and dispositions to organize and provide instruction at the appropriate school level for the study of global connections and interdependence.

Civic Ideals and Practices: Social studies teachers should possess the knowledge, capabilities, and dispositions to organize and provide instruction at the appropriate school level for the study of Civic Ideals and Practices.

NATIONAL EDUCATIONAL TECHNOLOGY FOUNDATION STANDARDS FOR STUDENTS

http://cnets.iste.org/sfors.htm

- Basic operations and concepts: Students demonstrate a sound understanding of the nature and operation of technology systems. Students are proficient in the use of technology.
- Social, ethical, and human issues: Students understand the ethical, cultural, and societal issues related to technology. Students practice responsible use of technology systems, information, and software. Students develop positive attitudes toward technology uses that support lifelong learning, collaboration, personal pursuits, and productivity.
- Technology productivity tool: Students use technology tools to enhance learning, increase productivity, and promote creativity. Students use productivity

tools to collaborate in constructing technology-enhanced models, preparing publications, and producing other creative works.

- Technology communications tools: Students use telecommunications to collaborate, publish, and interact with peers, experts, and other audiences. Students use a variety of media and formats to communicate information and ideas effectively to multiple audiences.
- Technology research tools: Students use technology to locate, evaluate, and collect information from a variety of sources. Students use technology tools to process data and report results. Students evaluate and select new information resources and technological innovations based on the appropriateness to specific tasks.
- Technology problem-solving and decision-making tools: Students use technology resources for solving problems and making informed decisions. Students employ technology in the development of strategies for solving problems in the real world.

NATIONAL CONTENT STANDARDS FOR VISUAL ARTS EDUCATION (©National Art Education Association)

www.getty.edu/artsednet/resources/scope/standards/

- Understanding and applying media, techniques, and processes.
- Using knowledge of structures and functions.
- Choosing and evaluating a range of subject matter, symbols, and ideas.
- Understanding the visual arts in relation to history and cultures.
- Reflecting upon and assessing the characteristics and merits of their work and the work of others.
- Making connections between visual arts and other disciplines.

Additional Suggestions for Case Analyses and Field Experiences

In a recent book, Allington and Johnston (2002) provided a review of studies that had explored the characteristics of exemplary teachers. This review describes specific personal characteristics of teachers (e.g., "stress resistance") and types of instructional beliefs and attitudes (e.g., "view learning as a social endeavor") that numerous studies had found significant to good teaching. Also important, of course, were the instructional practices and types of instructional talk found in the teachers' classrooms.

In this book we have recommended that, as part of your inquiry into content area literacy, you reflect on the cases presented, compare them to one another, and then link your inquiry on the written cases to observations of teachers in your own region. The purpose of observing is not to assess teachers you meet, but rather to get a sense of similarities and differences among teachers and teaching practices. You also may use resources, such as Allington and Johnson's text and others in this Content Area Handbook, to consider ways in which the teachers and teaching you have studied and observed compare to features other observers have identified as exemplary.

AREAS TO CONSIDER WHEN CONDUCTING OBSERVATIONS

1. How did the teacher start the lesson?
   - Arouse student interest
   - Connect to the student's background knowledge or prior learning
   - Etc.
2. How did the teacher teach the body of the lesson?
   - Strategies used
   - Lecture
   - Discussion
   - Whole group
   - Small group
   - Collaborative learning
   - Demonstration
   - Etc.

3. What materials were used in the lesson?
   - Textbooks
   - Computers
   - Videos
   - Transparencies
   - Worksheets
   - Concrete Objects
   - Etc.
4. What were students doing?
   - Listening
   - Answering questions
   - Discussing with each other
   - Writing
   - Etc.
5. What management and/or disciplinary techniques were used?
   - Rules posted
   - Rewards
   - Penalties
   - Flipping lights
   - Raised voice
   - Etc.
6. How did the teacher end the lesson?
   - Review
   - Assigned homework
   - Strategy
   - Bell rang
   - Etc.
7. How did the teacher assess and evaluate learning?
   - Oral questions
   - Quiz
   - Worksheet
   - Observation of student performance
   - Homework
   - Etc.

SUGGESTIONS FOR TEACHER INTERVIEWS

If you have the opportunity to interview a teacher after observing them, ask about what they did and why they did it. If you haven't observed, consider the following questions:

1. How do you start your lessons? Why?
2. How do you teach the body of your lessons? Why?
3. What materials do you typically use in your lessons? Why?
4. What do you expect of students?
5. What management and/or disciplinary techniques do you use? Why?
6. How do you end lessons?
7. How do you assess and evaluate student learning?

Case Analysis Chart (For Use With Cases in This Text)

Most interesting parts of the case:

What I liked best and my reason:

What I disagreed with (or what caused dissonance for me) and my reason:

Teacher, event, or situation it reminded me of in my own school experience:

What I saw that related to student motivation:

What I saw that related to student engagement:

Additional Suggestions for Case Analyses and Field Experiences

What I saw that related to classroom organization:

What I saw that related to teaching approaches:

What I saw that related to meeting student needs:

What I saw that related to incorporation of literacy in the content area:

Ideas or strategies I could apply in my own teaching situation:

Cross Case Analysis Chart (for Comparison of Cases in This Text)

Nature of Instruction in Case	Grade 6 Social Studies	Grade 7 Team	Grade 8 Social Studies and English	High School Biology	High School Math	High School English	English as a Second Language
Approaches to Reading							
Approaches to Writing							
Approaches to Classroom Discussion							
Approaches to Motivation/ Engagement							
Nature of Classroom Organization							
Other Category (Your Choice)							
Other Category (Your Choice)							

Additional References, Resources, and Websites

Additional References for Constructivism and Inquiry Learning

Brooks, J. G. & Brooks, M. G. (1999). *In search of understanding: The case for constructivist classrooms (Revised edition)*. Alexandria, VA: Association for Supervision and Curriculum Development

George, P. S., McEwin, C. K., & Jenkins, J. M. (2000). *The exemplary high school*. Fort Worth, TX: Harcourt College Publishers.

National Middle School Association. (1995). *This we believe: Developmentally responsive middle level schools*. Westerville, OH: Author.

MacLean, M. S. & Mohr, M. M. (1999). *Teacher-researchers at work*. Berkeley, CA: National Writing Project.

Shapiro, A. (2000). *Leadership for constructivist schools*. Lanham, MD: Scarecrow Press, Inc.

Additional References for Adolescent Literacy and Content Literacy

Alvermann, D.E., Hinchman, K.A., Moore, D. W., Phelps, S. F., & Waff, D.R. (Eds.) (1998). *Reconceptualizing the literacies in adolescents' lives*. Mahwah, NJ: Lawrence Erlbaum Associates, Inc.

International Reading Association. (2002). *To be a boy, to be a reader: Engaging teen and preteen boys in active literacy*. Newark, DE: Author.

Moje, E.B. (2000). *"All the stories that we have:" Adolescents' insights about literacy and learning in secondary schools*. Newark, DE: International Reading Association, Inc.

Rycik, J.A., & Irvin, J.L. (Eds.) (2001). *What adolescents deserve: A commitment to students' literacy learning*. Newark, DE: International Reading Association, Inc.

Spangenberg-Urbschat, K., & Pritchard, R. (Eds.) (1994). *Kids come in all languages: Reading instruction for ESL students*. Newark, DE: International Reading Association, Inc.

Tierney, R. J. & Readence, J.E. (2000). *Reading strategies and practices: A compendium* (5th ed.). Needham Heights, MA: Allyn & Bacon.

Vacca, R.T., & Vacca, J.L. (2002). *Content area reading: Literacy and learning across the curriculum* (7th ed.). Boston, MA: Allyn & Bacon.

Additional References for Effective Teaching

Allington, R. L., & Johnston, P. H. (2002). *Reading to learn: Lessons from exemplary fourth-grade classrooms*. New York: Guilford.

Brozo, W. G., & Simpson, M. L. (2003). *Readers, teachers, learners: Expanding literacy across the content areas, 4th ed.* Upper Saddle River, NJ: Merrill/Prentice Hall.

Ruddell, R. B., & Harris, P. (1989). A study of the relationship between influential teachers' prior knowledge and beliefs and teaching effectiveness: Developing higher-order thinking in content areas. In S. McCormick & J. Zutell (Eds.), *The 38th yearbook of the National Reading Conference* (pp. 461–472). Chicago: National Reading Conference.

Professional Organizations

International Reading Association

http://www.reading.org/
Headquarters Office
800 Barksdale Rd.
PO Box 8139
Newark, DE 19714–8139

The International Reading Association is a professional membership organization devoted to the promotion of high-level literacy. The website offers resources for professionals working to improve reading instruction and promote reading as a life-long habit. The site includes an archive of articles from reputable publications including *The Reading Teacher, Journal of Adolescent & Adult Literacy* and *Reading Today*. Literacy teachers can connect through the site's online discussion boards at http://www.reading.org/virtual/. These forums allow educators to discuss issues affecting literacy and to share ideas and resources that will further their professional development. Visitors to the site can also delve into topics related exclusively to adolescent literacy at http://www.reading.org/focus/adolescent.html. Here professionals working with adolescents can explore booklists highlighting top-quality literature for young adults, learn about professional development opportunities such as conferences and workshops across the country, and keep up to date on recent research findings. In addition, the website contains web links to other professional organizations devoted to quality reading instruction, an online bookstore containing recent publications, and information about the organization's multiple programs.

National Middle School Association

http://www.nmsa.org/
4151 Executive Parkway
Suite 300
Westerville, OH 43081
1–800–528-NMSA (6672)

The National Middle School Association, a professional membership organization, is committed to meeting the developmental and educational needs of young adults. It is the only national education association devoted exclusively to adolescent education. The website provides valuable resources and support to teachers, counselors, social workers, parents and others working with adolescents. It includes

Additional References, Resources, and Websites

research and articles related to issues affecting adolescents in addition to curriculum ideas, books, and teaching resources for enhancing adolescent education. In addition, the website contains links to other professional organizations dedicated to adolescent education, an online bookstore featuring current publications, and the most recent research findings in the field of adolescent education.

Additional Websites by Subject Area

- Art

  The National Endowment for the Arts
  http://www.arts.endow.gov/

- Educational Technology

  Texas Center for Educational Technolgoy
  www.tcet.unt.edu

- Foreign Language

  Links to Language Educator websites
  http://www.waterloo.k12.wi.us/whs/infocenter/
  edlang.htm

- Health

  The U.S. Surgeon General
  http://www.surgeongeneral.gov/

- History

  The History Channel
  http://historychannel.com
  Smithsonian Institution
  http://www.si.edu

- Language Arts

  National Public Radio
  http://www.npr.org/
  Public Broadcasting System
  http://www.pbs.org/

- Mathematics

  Cornell's Math Resources
  http://www.tc.cornell.edu/Ede/MathSciGateway/
  MegaMath
  http://www.c3.lanl.gov/mega-math/
  MathMagic
  http://forum.swarthmore.edu/mathmagic/

The Hub
http://hub.terc.edu/

- Music

  Music for Teachers
  www.m4t.org
  The National Association for Music Education
  www.menc.org
  K-12 Resources for Music Educators
  www.isd77.mn.us

- Science

  National Science Teachers Association
  http://www.nsta.org/
  Eisenhower National Clearinghouse
  http://www.enc.org/
  Official website of NASA
  http://www.nasa.gov/
  National Weather Service
  http://www.noaa.gov

- Social Studies

  Peace Corps
  http://www.peacecorps.gov/
  U.S. Census Bureau
  http://www.census.gov
  CNN Interactive
  http://www.cnn.com
  National Council for Social Studies
  http://www.ncss.org/
  Edsitement
  http://edsitement.neh.gov/

- Vocational Education

  U.S. Department of Labor Career Outlook
  http://stats.bls.gov/ocohome.htm
  Office of Vocational and Adult Education
  http://www.ed.gov/offices/OVAE/

Additional References, Resources, and Websites

Additional References for Teaching With the Internet

Wolgemuth, A. (1996). *Learning online: An educator's easy guide to the internet.* Arlington Heights, IL: IRI/SkyLight.

References

Alvermann, D.E. (2002). Effective literacy instruction for adolescents. *Journal of Literacy Research, 34*(2), 189–208.

Adams, R. (1972). *Watership Down.* New York: Macmillan Publishing.

Brubacher, J. W., Case, C. W., & Reagan, T. G. (1994). *Becoming a reflective educator: How to build a culture of inquiry in the schools.* Thousand Oaks, CA: Corwin Press.

Buss, F. L., & Cubias, D. (1991). *The Journey of the Sparrows.* New York: Lodestar Books.

Canfield, J., & Hansen, M. V. (1993). *Chicken Soup for the Soul.* Deerfield Beach, FL: Health Communications.

Gambrell, L. B. (1995). Motivation Matters. In W. M. Linkek & E. G. Sturtevant (Eds.), *Generations of Literacy* (pp. 2–24). Texas: The College Reading Association.

Gardner, J. (1971). *Grendel.* New York: Knopf.

Golding, W. (1954). *Lord of the Flies.* New York: Perigee.

Greenblat, C. S. (1988). *Designing Games and Simulations: An Illustrated Handbook.* Newbury Park, CA: Sage Publications.

Hardy, T. (1940). *The Return of the Native.* New York: The Modern Library.

Hynds, S. (1997). *On the Brink: Negotiating Literature and Life with Adolescents.* New York: Teachers College Press and the International Reading Association.

Jackson, P. W. (1968). *Life in Classrooms.* New York: Holt, Reinhart, & Winston.

McKenna, M. C., & Robinson, R. D. (1990). Content literacy: A definition and implications. *Journal of Reading, 34,* 184–186.

Mills, G.E. (2003). *Action research: A guide for the teacher researcher* (2nd ed.). Upper Saddle River, NJ: Merrill/Prentice Hall.

Moore, D. A. (1996). Contexts for literacy in secondary schools. In D. J. Leu, C. K. Kinzer & K. A. Hinchman (Eds.), *Literacies for the 21st Century: Research and Practice. Forty-fifth yearbook of the National Reading Conference.* Chicago, IL: National Reading Conference, Inc.

Moore, D. W., Bean, T. W., Birdyshaw, D., & Rycik, J. A. (1999). *Adolescent literacy: A position statement for the Commission on Adolescent Literacy of the International Reading Association.* Newark, DE: International Reading Association, Inc.

Supporting Young Adolescents' Literacy Learning: A Joint Position Paper of the International Reading Association and the National Middle School Association. Retrieved December 2002, from http://www.reading.org /positions/ supporting_young_adolesc.html.

National Council of Teachers of Mathematics (2000). *Principles and standards for school mathematics.* Reston, VA: National Council of Teachers of Mathematics.

Orwell, G. (1946). *Animal Farm.* New York: Harcourt, Brace and Company.

Ogle, D.M. (1986). K–W–L: A teaching model that develops active reading of expository text. *Reading Teacher, 39* (6), 564–570.

Philips, D. C., & Cleverley, J. (1995). *Visions of childhood: Influential models from Locke to Spock.* New York: Teachers College Press.

Richardson J. S., and Morgan, R. F. (2003). *Reading to learn in the content areas.* Belmont, CA: Wadsworth/Thomson Learning.

Sturtevant, E. G. (1996). *Lifetime influences on the literacy-related instructional beliefs of experienced high school history teachers: Two comparative case studies. Journal of Literacy Research 28*(2), 227–257.

Trigonometric Functions: 4.4 Sinusoidal Functions. Retrieved December 20, 2002 from http://jwbales.home.mindspring.com/precal/ part4.4html.

Vacca, R.T., & Rasinski, T.V. (1992). *Case studies in whole language.* New York: Harcourt Brace Jovanovich College Publishers.

Vacca, R. T., & Vacca, J. L. (2002). *Content Area Reading: Literacy and Learning Across the Curriculum,* 7e. Boston, MA: Allyn & Bacon.

White, S. (1999). The NAEP Reading Report Card: National and State Highlights. http://nces.ed.gov/pubsearch/pubsinfo.asp?=pubid1999479.

Zemelman, S., Daniels, H., & Hyde, A. A. (1993). *Best practice: New standards for teaching and learning in America's schools.* Portsmouth, NH: Heineman.

Index

Abstract reasoning abilities, 31
Academically gifted, 56
ADHD, 76
Adolescence
    International Reading
        Association (IRA) principle
        on literacy in, 6–7
    literacy and, 5–6
    literacy instruction and, 6
    references for literacy in, 161
    understanding, 5
After-reading strategies
    categorization and word
        maps, 132
    Directed Reading-Thinking
        Activity (DR-TA), 136–138
    discussion webs, 134
    graphic organizers, 146–152
    post-graphic organizer, 142
    progressive cinquain, 144
    progressive writing, 145
    save the last word for me, 145
    semantic mapping, 146
    Sketch to Stretch, 153
    summarization, 153
    think–pair–share, 154
    your own questions, 155
Agricultural education, national
        strategic plan and action
        agenda for, 157–158
Algebra standard for Grades
        6–12, 159–160
Anticipation guides, 142
Art, websites for, 174
Audiotapes, transcribing, 48–49
Autobiographical notebook, 100

Before-reading strategies
    brainstorming, 132
    categorization and word
        maps, 132

Directed Reading-Thinking
        Activity (DR-TA), 136–138
    LINK, 141
    graphic organizer, 146–152
    post-graphic organizer, 142
    prediction, 142
    PreP (pre reading plan), 143
    semantic mapping, 146–152
    think–pair–share, 154
    your own questions, 155
Best practice, 2
Biographical sketches, 110–111
Blended instruction, 28–39
Bonus questions, 86
Brainstorming, 19, 49, 59, 132

Case analysis chart, 121, 169–170
Cases, exploring inquiry
        learning through, 10
Case studies, 2, 67–70
Categorization maps, 137
Categorization strategy, 59, 74, 132
Character development, 26
Check sheets, 33
Choice, 101, 102–103
    opportunity for, 5
Choice instruction, 101
Class book, 110
Classroom arrangements, 43
Classroom learning, 37
Class schedules, modification
        of, 30
Class size, 92, 110
Collaboration between
        students, 110
Community involvement, 46
Computer, 22
Computer literacy, 4
Computer spreadsheets, 38
Concept and process reflection,
        131–132

Concept maps, 104
Conference, 112
Constructivism, 2
    references for, 172
Content area instruction, 31
Content-centered teacher, 70
Content literacy, 77
    defined, 4
    focus on, 3
    references for, 161
    teachers' responsibility in, 7–9
    views of, 4
Core subject teachers, 30
Cross-case analysis, 124–125
Cross-case comparison, 121–122
Cross-curriculum reading, 116
Curriculum
    inquiry-based social studies, 57
    joint, 44–45
    multi-dimensional, 45
    process oriented, 45
    textbook-based, 104

Data Analysis and Probability
        Standard for Grades
        6–12, 162
Debates, 18, 67
Dewey, John, 42
Dialogue journals, 112
Directed Reading-Thinking
        Activity (DR-TA), 107,
        120, 136–138
Discussion, 66–67, 97–98
Discussion webs, 134
Double entry journals, 135–136
Double-period class, 75–76
During-reading strategies
    categorization and word
        maps, 132
    Directed Reading-Thinking
        Activity (DR-TA), 136–138

During-reading strategies,
    continued
    double entry journals, 135–136
    insert, 138
    graphic organizer, 146–152
    post-graphic organizer, 142
    save the last word for me, 145
    semantic mapping, 146–152
    think–pair–share, 154
    your own questions, 155

Educational technology, websites
    for, 174
Effective teaching, references
    for, 173–174
E-mail listserves, 119
English
    in high school, 92–106
    integrated civics and, 40–58
    national standards for
        education, 40, 92,
        157–159
English for Speakers of Other
    Languages (ESOL), 31,
    37, 107–120
    programs for, 30
Expectation outlines, 142
Experimentation, 64
Exploration of science
    concepts, 62
Expository text
    DR-TA for, 137–138
    K-W-L strategy for, 139–141

Faculty collaboration, 30
First-draft writing, 112
Foreign language, websites
    for, 174
Free-choice reading, 45

Geometry standard for Grades
    6–12, 161
Gifted and talented programs, 41
Graphic organizers, 50–52,
    146–152
    cause/effect text structure, 151
    compare/contrast text
        structure, 150
    descriptive text structure, 148

problem/solution text
    structure, 152
sequential text structure, 149
Group in-class assignments,
    85–88
Grouping arrangements, 20–22
Group work, 45
Guest speakers, 55–56

Hands on learning, 37, 38, 63
Health, websites for, 174
Higher-order thinking, 80
High school
    biology in, 59–74
    English in, 92–106
    mathematics in, 75–91
History. *See also* Social studies
    sixth grade world, 11–27
    websites for, 174

Immersion, 111–112
Inclusion, 30, 37
Independent reading
    project, 54
Independent thinkers, 80
Individualized Education
    Program (IEP), 101
Individualized reading, 44–45
Informal assessment, 79
Informational text, DR-TA
    for, 137–138
Inquiry, teaching as, 123–124
Inquiry-based social studies
    curriculum, 57
Inquiry learning
    exploring, through cases, 10
    references for, 172
INSERT (Interactive notation
    system to effective
    reading and thinking),
    28, 39, 138
Instruction. *See also* Learning
    blended, 28–39
    choice, 101
    content area, 31
    small group, 21, 41, 49, 50, 81
    strategy, 101
    student-centered, 30, 61, 62,
        70, 71

whole-class, 21, 49, 63–64. 66,
    73, 78, 81, 113–117
Instructional decisions, making,
    17–18
Instructional observation,
    format for, 125, 126
Integrated civics and English,
    40–58
Integrated curriculum, 56
Interdisciplinary projects, 28–39,
    37, 38
International Reading
    Association, 173
    Commission on Adolescent
        Literacy, 158–159
    standards for English
        language arts, 149–150
Internet, 65. *See also* Websites
    references for teaching with, 175

Joint curriculum, development
    of, 44–45
Journals, 112
    dialogue, 112
    double entry, 135–136
    response, 99, 102

K-W-L strategy, 18, 19, 40, 58,
    104, 124, 132, 139–141

Lab write-ups, 66
Language, uses of, 49
Language arts
    IRA/NCTE standards for,
        158–159
    websites for, 165
Learning. *See also* Instruction
    classroom, 37
    hands on, 37, 38, 63
    inquiry, 10, 170
    standards of, 57
    strategic, 98–99
    text-based, 64
Learning disabilities, 76
Lectures, 62, 73, 77
Lifelong reader, 93
Linear model, 86
LINK (List, Inquire, Note,
    Know), 11, 141

Literacy, 38
  adolescence and, 5–7, 172
  content, 3, 4, 7–9, 77, 172
  focus on, 64–65
  instruction in, 6
  scientific, 4, 64
Literary learning, supports
  , 123

Magnet programs, 41
Mainstreaming, 37, 93
Mathematics
  in high school, 75–91
  national standard for education
    in, 77, 90, 160–163
  websites for, 174–175
Measurement standard for
  Grades 6–12, 174
Memorization-style teaching, 62
Metacognitive abilities, 128
Mini-lessons, 54, 95, 112
Motivation, 72
Multicultural day, 118
Multi-dimensional curriculum
  integration, 45
Music, websites for, 175

Narrative text and stories,
  DRTA for, 136
Narrative writing, 49
National Academy for the
  Advancement of
  Sciences, 89
National Assessment of
  Educational Progress
  (NAEP) Reading Report
  Card, 6
National Content Standards for
  Visual Arts Education, 166
National Council for the Social
  Studies: National
  Standards for Social
  Studies Teachers, 164–165
National Council of Teachers of
  English (NCTE), 97
  standards for English
    education, 40, 92, 158–159
National Council of Teachers of
  Mathematics Standards

(NCTM), 75, 77, 90,
  160–163
National Educational
  Technology Foundation
  Standards for Students,
  165–166
National Middle School
  Association, 173
National Reading Conference, 123
National standards, 157–166
  development of, 4
  in English, 40, 92, 157–160
  in English for Speakers of
    Other Languages, 107
  in mathematics, 75, 77,
    160–163
  in science, 59, 163–164
  in social studies, 28, 40,
    164–165
  for visual arts, 28
Note-taking, 70, 77, 99, 126
Number and Operations
  Standard for
  Grades 6–12, 160

Observations, 64
  areas to consider when
    conducting, 167–168
On-task behavior, 79
Oral communication, 38, 49
  in sixth grade world history
    class, 20
Oral reflections, 31
Organization, 128
Outlining, 99

Pairs, 78–79
Parent involvement, 46
Partner in-class assignments,
  85–88
Planning and instructional
  decision-making, 63–64
Portfolios, 22, 54
Post-graphic organizer, 140
Prediction, 28, 142
PreP (Pre reading plan), 75, 143
Pre-reading strategies. *See*
  Before-reading strategies
Process oriented curriculum, 45

Professional development, 24–26,
  37, 57, 70–72, 118–119
  framework for, 126
Professional satisfaction,
  103–104
Progressive cinquain, 91, 144
Progressive movement, 42, 57
Progressive writing, 120, 145
Published reading materials,
  students personal
  connection to, 116

Question generation/answer
  explanation, 129

Reading. *See also* After-reading
  strategies; Before-reading
  strategies; During-reading
  strategies
  cross-curriculum, 116
  free-choice, 45
  individualized, 44–45
  linking writing assignments
    and, 113–117
  in sixth grade world history
    class, 20
Real world applications, 62, 77
Response journal, 99, 102
Risk-taking environment, 14
Role-playing, 31, 67
Rubrics, 54

Save the last word for me
  strategy, 28, 39, 145
Scaffolding, 78, 96–97, 99, 101
Scheduling, 72–73
Science, 164
  exploration of, 62
  national standards for
    education in, 59,
    157–159
Scientific literacy, 4, 64
Scoring guides, 84–85
Semantic mapping, 40,
  146–152
Sensitive topics, 67–70
Service-learning opportunity,
  31, 38
Shared planning period, 56

Simulations, 32–35, 37
    social studies, 31
    whole-team, 31
Sixth grade world history, 11–27
    classroom, 14–16
    grouping arrangements,
        20–22
    instruction in, 16–24
    making instructional
        decisions, 17–18
    reading, writing, and oral
        communication in, 20
    special projects and
        assignments, 22–24
    teaching and learning
        strategies, 18–19
    textbooks and materials, 20
Sketch to stretch strategy, 58, 153
Small group instruction, 21, 41,
    49, 50, 81
Social studies, 164. *See also*
        History
    inquiry-based curriculum in, 57
    national standards for, 28, 40,
        164–165
    simulation, 31
Special education, 30, 31, 93, 101
Special needs, 70
Special projects and
    assignments, 22–24
Spin-off topics, 44
Sponge activity, 95
S. S. Toy Company Project:
    Grade Seven, 28–39
Standardized testing, effects of,
    26–27
Standards of learning, 57
State-mandated tests, 90
Strategic teaching and learning,
    98–99
Strategy instruction, 101
Student-centered instruction,
    30, 61, 62, 70, 71

Student council, 26
Student generated
        elaborations, 128
Student motivation, 15
Student presentations, 18
Student procrastination, 24
Student reflections, 35–36
Student responsibility, 73
Subject area, websites for,
    174–175
Summarization, 65, 74, 75,
    91, 153
Summary chart, 52
Sustained silent writing, 106

Tally sheet, 34–35
Teacher action research, 124, 125
Teacher-centered transmission
    approach, 129
Teacher interviews, suggestions
    for, 166
Teacher researcher, taking
    stance as, 124–126
Teachers' responsibility, in
    content literacy, 7–9
Teaching
    as inquiry, 123–124
    with the Internet, 175
    memorization-style, 62
    references for effective, 163
    strategic, 98–99
    strategies in, 73
    team, 41, 42, 43, 46, 54–56, 61
    vocabulary, 96–97
Team planning, 89
Team teaching, 41, 42, 43, 46,
    54–56, 61
Technology
    special projects using, 118
    standards for education,
        165–166
Text-based learning, 64
Textbook-based curriculum, 104

Textbooks and materials, 20
Text summarization, 129
Think aloud strategy, 19, 98–99
Think-Pair-Share Activity, 78–79
Timeline activity, 18
Timeline expansion, 15–16
Time management, 73
Transcribed interviews, 49–50

Venn diagrams, 19
Videotape editing, 46
Visual arts education, national
        content standards for, 166
Vocabulary, teaching, 96–97
Volunteerism, 46–52

Webs, 19
    discussion, 132
Websites, 119. *See also* Internet
    by subject area, 174–175
Whole-class instruction, 21, 49, 73
    books in, 113–117
    discussion in, 66, 78
    exercises in, 81
    mini-lessons in, 63–64
    sessions in, 64
    simulations in, 31
    visits in, 46
Writing
    development of, 99–101
    first-draft, 112
    linking reading assignments
        and, 113–117
    narrative, 49
    progressive, 120, 145
    revising, 112
    in sixth grade world history
        class, 20
    sustained silent, 106
Written communication, 31, 66

Your own questions strategy, 92,
    106, 155